Healthy Food
Young ^for^ Children

Expert advice from:
Alison McLaughlin, MSc, MA

Cover design by
Mary Cartwright

Food photography by
Howard Allman

Food preparation and styling by
Dagmar Vesely

American editor:
Carrie Armstrong

US food consultant:
Barbara Tricinella

Healthy Food
Young Children
for

Henny Fordham

Illustrated by Shelagh McNicholas
and Ruth Russell

Designed by Joanne Kirkby
and Laura Hammonds

Edited by Felicity Brooks
and Emma Helbrough

Contents

Lunch recipes

Main meals

Drinks and desserts

Useful information

Introduction

The food that children eat provides their bodies with the energy and nutrients they need to grow and function efficiently, so the more nutritious and balanced their diet is, the better their bodies – and brains – will work. Research shows that childhood diets can also have a huge impact on long-term health and fitness prospects, so encouraging children to eat well from an early age really is vital.

But when you are busy it can be hard to provide a varied and healthy diet day after day, especially if children are picky about what they eat, and it's all too easy to resort to ready-made meals, fast food and store-bought snacks, which are not usually the healthiest options.

Children are more likely to be adventurous with food if they have helped grow, pick or prepare it themselves.

As well as a healthy diet, children need plenty of exercise. You can find out more on pages 42 to 44.

Did you know?

Studies have shown that behavior and concentration levels are markedly higher in children who have eaten a healthy breakfast.

Recent research has concluded that children whose diet includes plenty of fruit, vegetables and fish are much less likely to develop asthma and allergies.

A recent scientific study has confirmed a link between specific food additives and hyperactive behavior in young children.

This book offers lots of ideas, suggestions, tips and tactics for how to get children to eat well, without your having to spend hours in the kitchen. The first half brings together information and advice about nutrition and children's diets, based on the latest research. The second half contains ideas and recipes for simple, healthy meals, snacks and drinks. The overall goal is to help you get children to enjoy good food and learn to make healthy choices for themselves.

A healthy diet

Eating healthy doesn't have to mean hours
of preparation; it doesn't have to be boring, and
it doesn't mean children can never have treats or
sweet things. It is about balance and variety – and
remembering that a few small changes in children's
diets, if needed, can make a big difference to their
overall health in the long term. This section looks
in detail at the different kinds of foods that
make up a healthy diet for children.

At a glance

Try to get children to eat at least five servings
of fruits and vegetables every day.

Try to provide whole-grain rice, bread and cereal for
about half of all 'Grain' servings each day.

It's important that children get three servings of dairy a day
– milk, low-fat cheese and yogurt are all good choices.

Try to get children to eat more nuts, beans and fish.

What is a balanced diet?

A great deal of research has gone into what makes a balanced diet and the information here comes from studies by the World Health Organization and various food standards agencies, including the USDA. The different kinds of foods children need to eat each day and the proportions they require are shown below.

Useful tip
To help you remember these proportions, you can print out this diagram from the Usborne Quicklinks Website (see page 123).

One-third of a child's diet should be fruits and vegetables and one-third should be grains.

One-third should be shared between dairy products and protein, with just a few sweet and fatty foods.

Fruits and vegetables

Grains (bread, other cereals, rice, potatoes, pasta, etc.)

Milk and dairy products

Protein (meat, fish and beans)

Sugary and fatty foods

A banana counts as one serving of fruit.

The chart below shows the average amounts of each food group that children should be eating each day.

Food type	Age 2 to 5 years	Age 6 to 10 years
Grains	6 servings (3-5 oz.)	9-10 servings (5-6 oz.)
Fruits	2 servings (1-1 ½ cups)	3 servings (1 ½ cups)
Vegetables	3 servings (1-1 ½ cups)	4 servings (2-2 ½ cups)
Milk, yogurt, cheese	2-3 servings (2 cups)	2-3 servings (2-3 cups)
Meat, beans, fish, eggs	2 servings (2-4 oz.)	2 servings (4-6 oz.)

What is a serving?

As a guideline, each item listed below is an example of one serving of the different kinds of foods.

Grains:

- 3 tablespoons breakfast cereal (without added sugar)
- 1 thick slice of bread
- 2 heaped tablespoons boiled rice
- 3 heaped tablespoons boiled pasta
- 2 egg-sized potatoes

Find out more about grains and carbohydrates on page 12.

Fruits and vegetables:

- 1 glass of fruit juice
- 1 apple, banana or pear
- 1 orange
- 2 halves of canned peaches
- 1 handful of berries like raspberries or strawberries
- 1 slice of melon
- 1 tablespoon raisins
- 3 dried apricots
- 1 carrot
- 3 tablespoons cooked carrots, peas or corn
- 1 cereal bowl of salad leaves
- 2 inch piece of cucumber

There's more about fruits and vegetables on page 10.

Dairy products:

- 1 small piece of cheese (1 oz.)
- 1 glass of milk (5 1/2 oz., 2/3 cup)
- 1 carton of yogurt (5 oz.)

Find information about dairy products on page 16.

Protein:

- a piece of meat, poultry or fish about the size of the palm of the child's hand
- 3 tablespoons cooked beans
- 1 tablespoon peanut butter
- 1/2 oz. nuts or seeds
- 1 egg

Discover more about protein on page 18.

Protein sources

Protein is vital for growth, and some parents worry that their children don't get enough, but protein comes from a range of sources and as long as children eat a variety of dairy produce, some meat, fish, eggs, nuts, beans, and/or soy products, they are likely to be getting enough.

Find out why we should all avoid eating too much junk food, processed food, sugar, salt and certain kinds of fat on pages 25–33.

Fruit is generally at its most nutritious in its natural state.

Fruits and vegetables

There's growing scientific evidence that eating at least five servings of fruits and vegetables each day can help reduce the risk of heart disease and some cancers in later life, so if you can get a child to choose an apple, banana or carrot as a snack, you've achieved one goal of healthy eating.

As well as essential vitamins and minerals, fruits and vegetables contain phytochemicals, which give the food its color and flavor and have been shown to help reduce the risk of a number of diseases.

Children may enjoy blending up fruit in milkshakes and smoothies. (See page 63 for some ideas.)

Five-a-day in disguise

Most children will like at least one fruit and vegetable, but it can be difficult to build up to the recommended five servings. One way to introduce a wider variety is to disguise vegetables by blending them into sauces and soups. Once you have found a vegetable, for example corn, that children like, try adding something else such as peas or chopped carrots. It doesn't matter how small you cut something up, it is still nutritionally valuable.

When you go shopping, encourage young children to choose a new kind of fruit or vegetable to try.

Is fresh best?

The answer is yes, if the fruits and vegetables really are fresh. Limp vegetables and wrinkly fruits that have been sitting around for weeks may have lower levels of some vitamins than frozen fruits and vegetables that have been frozen soon after picking.

Try to buy fruits and vegetables in an unprocessed state.

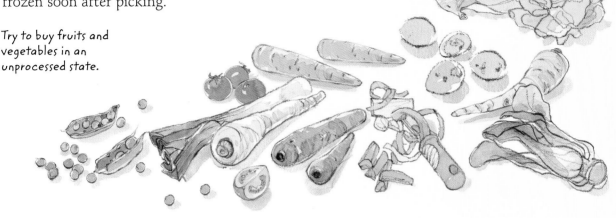

When choosing produce, be aware that most supermarket fruits and vegetables have been processed in some way. Make sure you wash supermarket produce under running water before eating it. Produce has been handled by many people on its way to you, and may also have pesticides or other chemical residues from the farm. If possible, buy fruits and vegetables with their skins or outer leaves still on. Though they take a little longer to prepare, their nutritional value will be higher. Vegetables should be eaten as soon as possible after you buy them, but if you need to store any, you can store most in a cool, dark place, such as the bottom of the refrigerator, to prevent sprouting, mold growth and rotting.

Did you know?

Eating apples regularly has been linked with a reduced risk of asthma and diabetes.

Eating tomatoes is thought to help reduce the risk of some cancers.

Carrots contain carotene which protects against some diseases.

Does cooking destroy vitamins?

It does destroy some – especially vitamin C – but it also breaks down the cellulose structure of fruits and vegetables and this makes the food more digestible. The best way to retain the vitamins in vegetables is to steam them. Some nutrients will still be leached into the water, but you could keep it for making soups and sauces.

If you don't have a steamer, use a metal sieve or colander over a pan of boiling water with a lid on top.

All about carbs

Carbohydrates (often known as 'carbs') are what give children's bodies the energy to fuel them through the day. Foods in the 'Grains' food group contain the most carbs and include bread, potatoes, pasta, rice, yams, oats, noodles, breakfast cereals, millet, barley, rye and beans. Carbohydrates (in particular whole grains) should form the basis of a healthy diet and account for at least a third of what children eat.

It's a good idea to plan meals around healthy carbohydrates.

As well as energy, carbohydrates provide:

• B vitamins, which help the body to use energy.

• Calcium for strong teeth and bones.

• Iron for healthy blood cells.

Starches and sugars

Carbohydrates come in two forms. The first are known as complex, or starchy, carbohydrates. It's the starch in flour that thickens sauces, the starch in oats that forms oatmeal when heated with water, and the starch in rice that makes the water turn cloudy when soaked in water. The other form of carbohydrates are simple carbohydrates or sugars. These occur naturally in fruit and milk and are good for you. The refined sugar that you buy in packages and that is found in cakes, cookies, drinks and other processed foods should only be eaten in small quantities.

Pasta is a versatile carbohydrate and can be served hot or cold. See pages 80–83 for some recipes.

Fuel and fiber

Starchy carbohydrates in foods such as bread, rice, pasta and potatoes provide glucose which is the most important energy source for muscles and other tissues and organs, including the brain. It's vital for children to have a regular intake of starchy foods for their bodies to function at their best. Children also need starchy foods for fiber to keep their digestive systems healthy and to help prevent constipation.

Potatoes are a source of fiber, protein, B vitamins, iron and vitamin C. Their skins contain potassium and fiber.

Starchy carbohydrates provide children with the energy they need to keep them moving.

Dried pasta is easy to store. It is a good source of energy and also contains some vitamins and minerals.

Fiber facts

There are two kinds of fiber: soluble and insoluble. Soluble fiber can be digested fully and helps reduce cholesterol in the blood. Cholesterol is a type of fat made by the body. It is essential for good health, but high levels can lead to heart disease and strokes in later life. Good sources of soluble fiber include oats, and beans such as lentils.

Insoluble fiber, also called dietary fiber, helps other food and waste products move through the digestive system easily. Whole-grain bread and breakfast cereals, brown rice, fruit and vegetables all contain dietary fiber.

Bread provides energy, is low in fat, a good source of fiber and protein and contains calcium, iron and vitamins.

Useful tip

Encourage children to eat more whole-grain bread by putting some in a basket on the table at mealtimes.

Choosing whole-grain foods

When rice and wheat go through a factory refining process to make white rice and white flour (for bread, pasta and so on), the high fiber parts from the grains are removed, along with important nutrients. The resulting foods are less nutritious than their brown, or whole-grain, counterparts.

Studies show that eating whole-grain foods helps children stay healthy if combined with exercise and a balanced diet. High in fiber and complex carbohydrates, they help children feel fuller for longer and also help to keep glucose levels up, which makes them feel happy. Here are some more benefits of eating whole-grain foods:

- Whole-grain foods often contain less fat and sugar.
- They are a good source of protein and vitamins.
- Their high fiber content can help prevent constipation.

A whole grain of wheat is made up of three parts.

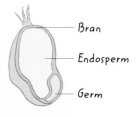

Bran

Endosperm

Germ

The bran and the germ, which are high in fiber and nutrients, are removed in processing to make white flour.

Did you know?

If the ingredients list 'whole wheat', 'wholemeal' or 'whole corn' as the first ingredient, the product is a whole-grain food.

Brown rice

Whole corn kernels, sold for popping

Whole grains, including rolled oats

Whole-wheat pasta

Whole-wheat bread

Nutrition experts suggest that we should all make at least half of the carbohydrates we eat whole grains and the pictures above show some major sources. The list at the top of the facing page shows what counts as a serving.

Whole grain vs. fortified

White bread is often fortified (by law in some countries including the UK, USA and Canada). This means that nutrients lost during refining are added back to the flour. Although it is recognized that this can benefit children's overall health, experts agree it's better to eat whole-grain bread with nutrients in place, rather than white bread with some added. Even after fortification, white bread doesn't contain all the nutrients and fiber of whole-grain bread.

Each of the following counts as one serving:

- *2 heaped tablespoons cooked brown rice*

- *3 heaped tablespoons whole-grain pasta*

- *1 medium slice of whole-grain bread*

- *3 tablespoons whole-grain cereal*

- *2–3 cups of plain popcorn*

Whole-grain foods keep children filled up and full of energy for longer.

- *Provide a plate of brown and white toast with different favorite spreads.*

- *Add barley to stews and casseroles.*

- *Try 'white' whole-grain bread if children refuse to eat brown.*

- *Offer whole-grain cereals or oatmeal for breakfast.*

- *Add oatmeal to cookie recipes and desserts.*

- *Buy whole-grain muffins or pita bread.*

Introducing more brown

If children are used to 'white' foods, they are often reluctant to try more 'brown', but this really is a change worth making if you need to. Below and on the right are some ideas and tactics to try for introducing more whole-grain foods.

Make half and half white and brown sandwiches.

Dentists agree that milk is one of the few drinks that is safe to drink between meals. One 5 ½ oz. (²/₃ cup) glass of milk contains:

• About half the daily requirements for calcium, phosphorus and vitamin B2.

• About one-third of the protein, potassium and iodine and all of the vitamin B12.

• Small amounts of vitamins A, B1 and B6, also niacin, folate, zinc, magnesium and Omega-3 fatty acids. (See page 19 and 22 to 24).

Dairy products

Dairy products such as milk, cheese and yogurt contain high levels of calcium, which children need for the healthy development of their bones and teeth. They also provide protein, vitamins and other useful nutrients. Nutritionists recommend that children eat three servings of dairy a day.

Calcium for bone health

Research has found that many children and young adults don't get enough calcium. Over time, this can increase the risk of developing brittle bone disease (osteoporosis) in later life. Our bodies absorb most calcium during childhood, so it's vital that children eat enough calcium-rich foods. Dairy produce is the highest source of calcium. Vegetables contain it in lower quantities.

Activities such as skating, walking, running, soccer and dancing help strengthen bones.

Children need to have whole (full-fat) milk until they are at least two years old because they may not get enough calories (needed in particular for brain development) from low-fat milk. At age two, check with your child's doctor to see if they recommend switching to low-fat milk. The doctor will base their recommendation on the child's weight, activity level and overall nutrition.

Useful yogurt

Natural yogurt, made by fermenting milk with bacteria, is very nutritious and provides calcium, B vitamins, protein, energy and beneficial intestinal bacteria. Most yogurt is 'live' (whatever it says on the label). This means the bacteria that are used to make it are still alive in the yogurt and some are responsible for the production of vitamin K.

Useful tip

Flavored store-bought yogurts may contain a lot of sugar. Buy natural yogurt and add your own flavors such as honey, puréed fruit, or some vanilla.

Live culture yogurt has a mild flavor and is believed to aid digestion.

Remember that each of these counts as one of the three servings of dairy children need each day:

• One glass (that is about $2/3$ cup or 5 $1/2$ oz.) of milk

• One small carton (5 oz.) of yogurt

Cheese

The calcium in cheese could help prevent colon cancer, as well as osteoporosis, and may help regulate blood pressure. A recent report also found that eating cheese may help prevent tooth decay by increasing the amount of saliva, helping to neutralize acid which erodes tooth enamel. The high calcium and phosphorus content of cheese may also help replace some of the minerals in tooth enamel.

• A small (1 oz.) piece of cheese

Let children try some different kinds of cheeses and talk about which flavors and textures they prefer.

Protein

Protein is essential for muscle growth and children require increasing amounts from infancy to adolescence. It is found in meat, poultry, fish, eggs, milk and cheese and also in cereals, bread, nuts, beans, soy products such as tofu or vegetarian products containing mycoprotein (from fungi).

Meat protein

Meat contains essential fatty acids or EFAs, as well as the minerals zinc and iron. EFAs are 'essential' because the human body needs them to function and they can only be obtained from food – the body can't manufacture them. Although protein is a vital part of a healthy diet, animal protein (from meat, fish, eggs and cheese) should only make up ten percent of what is on children's plates.

Refrigerate or freeze meat as soon as possible after you buy it. (See page 47 for advice on storing raw meat).

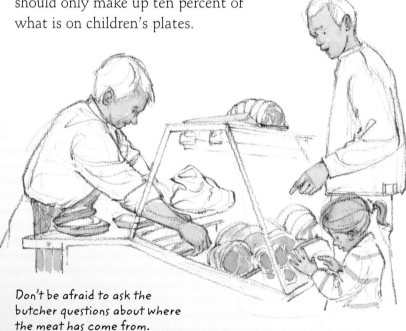

Don't be afraid to ask the butcher questions about where the meat has come from.

Useful tip

Good supermarkets and butchers should be able to tell you how their meat has been farmed, so you can make an informed choice about what you buy.

Farm animals are often reared in cramped conditions and routinely fed antibiotics. The long-term effects of eating meat from animals kept in this way are not known. Organic and free-range meat is often more expensive, but it's healthier to give children a small amount of good quality meat than a larger serving from a factory farm.

Eggs and beans

Eggs are a good choice as part of a healthy diet and there's no recommended limit on how many children should eat. Eggs are high in protein and contain iodine, B vitamins and vitamins A, D and E (see pages 22 to 24). They also contain cholesterol. Despite what was previously thought, it's now known that eating foods high in cholesterol doesn't raise blood cholesterol (though diets high in saturated fat can).

Beans are edible seeds that grow in pods. They are a low-fat source of protein, fiber, vitamins and minerals. Beans are also an excellent source of protein for both vegetarians and meat-eaters.

A hard-boiled egg is ideal for breakfast.

Scrambled eggs are good for a light lunch.

Omelets make a fast, nutritious evening meal.

Canned beans add texture and flavor to soups and casseroles.

Some bean varieties:
- runner beans
- chickpeas
- fava beans
- kidney beans
- butter beans
- navy beans
- black-eyed peas
- garden peas
- lentils

What's so good about fish?

Fish is a good source of protein, iron, selenium and iodine, as well as vitamins A and D. White fish, such as cod and haddock are very low in fat. Oily fish and some shellfish, such as crabs and mussels, are an important source of Omega-3 fatty acids which have been associated with helping guard against heart disease, boosting the immune system and combating skin problems. Some scientists also claim they help maintain brain function and aid concentration.

Nutritionists advise that children should eat oily fish such as salmon, mackerel and sardines twice a week.

It's healthier to poach, bake or grill fish. Fried fish is high in fat, especially if covered in batter or crumbs.

Bananas contain potassium, zinc, iron, folic acid, calcium, B6 and fiber and are good for digestion.

Garlic reduces cholesterol and blood fats, and also has anti-bacterial and anti-fungal properties.

Oatmeal is the best breakfast cereal. It reduces blood cholesterol and the risk of heart disease and strokes.

Superfoods

Scientists are continually testing foods to discover what they contain and how to use this knowledge in the fight against disease. 'Superfoods' is the name given to foods that have been found to be special in some way from a nutritional point of view. They may contain high levels of certain vitamins, or a range of health enhancing nutrients.

Old beliefs, new proof

The healing powers of foods have been known for centuries but are being treated with a new respect, as their chemical properties are being more clearly understood. The belief that fish is good for your brain has been given new credence with the discovery of Omega-3; the aptly named herb sage can help in the treatment of Alzheimer's disease, and berries have been found to contain high levels of antioxidants that help guard against disease.

The antioxidants in berries boost children's immunity against infection and are said to assist brain development.

Nutritious nuts and seeds

Nuts and seeds are little powerhouses of nutrition. They contain high levels of fiber and protein, as well as many vitamins and minerals. Nuts also contain monounsaturated fat, which can help reduce the amount of cholesterol in the blood. (See pages 30 to 31 for more about this.) As they are high in fat, they are very filling as a snack. Seeds such as sunflower, pumpkin, sesame and poppy add texture and flavor to salads, breakfast cereals and bread.

Apples contain pectin and vitamin C, which reduces cholesterol and protects against the effects of pollution.

If you buy nuts in their shells, older children may enjoy cracking them.

Safety point

Whole nuts should not be given to children under five as they can choke on them. Nuts are also common causes of food allergies. See pages 120–121.

Avocados are rich in potassium, which helps combat tiredness, depression and poor digestion.

About antioxidants

Oxidation is a process that, in the human body, produces chemicals called free radicals. These chemicals gradually destroy the structure of cells and it's this deterioration that has been linked to a variety of diseases, including heart disease and certain cancers. Antioxidants are substances in foods that search for and disable free radicals. These foods are all high in antioxidants:

Cauliflower, cabbage and broccoli contain iron, vitamin C, chlorophyll and sulfur, which help boost the immune system to protect against disease.

- prunes
- raisins
- blueberries
- blackberries
- strawberries
- raspberries
- plums

- oranges
- red grapes
- cherries
- kiwi fruit
- pink grapefruit
- cabbage
- spinach

- Brussels sprouts
- alfalfa sprouts
- broccoli
- beets
- red peppers
- onions
- eggplants

Citrus fruits contain fiber, potassium, vitamin C and carotenoids, which also stimulate the immune system.

Vitamins and minerals

Vitamins and minerals are essential for health but the
human body cannot manufacture them. They have to
come from food, and from sunlight. A balanced, healthy
diet should provide all the vitamins, minerals and other
nutrients that children need. However, if a child has a very
restricted diet, or health problems, supplements may be
needed, though this should be at the recommendation of
a doctor or dietician. These charts show what vitamins
and minerals do and which foods are their main sources.

Vitamin	What does it do?	Sources
Vitamin A (Retinol/Beta carote)	Maintains healthy skin and mucous membranes (lining of digestive system and lungs). Needed for normal growth, vision and by immune system.	Liver, whole milk, cheese, butter, carrots, dark green leafy vegetables, orange fruit, such as mango, peach and apricot. Margarine is fortified with vitamin A in some countries.
Vitamin D (Cholecalciferol)	Made by action of sun on the skin, vitamin D helps control calcium absorption and is vital for absorption of phosphorus.	Sunlight. Also occurs naturally in meat, oily fish, eggs and butter. Margarine is fortified with vitamin D and it is added to some cereals.
Vitamin E	Acts as an antioxidant and is required to protect cells against damage by free radicals. May reduce risk of some types of cancers and heart disease.	Richest sources are vegetable oils including soy, corn and olive oil. Also found in whole-grain cereals, nuts, seeds and eggs.
Vitamin C (Ascorbic acid)	Required for normal structure and function of skin, cartilage, bone and nervous system. Also for iron absorption, particularly from plant sources.	Foods from plant sources, such as apples, berries, citrus fruits, potatoes, green vegetables. Fresh milk and liver also contain small amounts.
Vitamin K	Essential for clotting of blood and also required for normal bone structure.	Green leafy vegetables such as broccoli and spinach, cereals and vegetable oils.

Vitamin	What does it do?	Sources
Vitamin B1 (Thiamin)	Needed to release energy from carbohydrates. It is involved in normal functioning of nervous system and heart.	Whole grains, nuts and meat, especially pork. White and brown flour and many breakfast cereals are fortified with thiamin.
Vitamin B2 (Riboflavin)	Required to release energy from protein, carbohydrates and fat, for the metabolism of iron and to maintain healthy skin and mucous membranes.	Milk, eggs, fortified breakfast cereals, liver, green vegetables, rice and mushrooms. UV light destroys vitamin B2, so keep these foods out of direct sunlight.
Vitamin B3 (Niacin)	Required for release of energy from food, for healthy skin and mucus membranes and for the functioning of the nervous system.	Beef, pork, chicken, wheat and corn flour, fish, nuts, potatoes, pasta and yeast extract. Eggs, milk, cheese and yogurt help the body synthesize vitamin B3.
Vitamin B6	Essential for the metabolism of protein. It is also involved in the metabolism and transport of iron.	Found in a variety of foods: beef, fish and poultry are rich sources. Also occurs in eggs, whole grains and some vegetables.
Vitamin B12 (Cobalamin)	Required for normal cell division, for making red blood cells and to keep the nervous system healthy. It also helps to release energy from food and is needed to process folate.	Good sources include meat, salmon, cod, milk, cheese, eggs, yeast extract, some fortified breakfast cereals, and certain algae such as seaweed. Vegans need to take it as a supplement.
Folate	Essential for normal cell division, nervous system and formation of blood cells. Helps reduce the risk of neural tube defects such as spina bifida in unborn babies.	Found in liver, yeast extract, orange juice and green leafy vegetables. Breakfast cereals and bread are often fortified with folic acid – the synthetic form of folate.

Foods from different food groups provide different vitamins and minerals.

Mineral	What does it do?	Sources
Calcium	Builds and strengthens bones and teeth. Also needed for blood clotting and functioning of nerves and muscles.	Milk, cheese, yogurt, canned fish (when bones included), dark green leafy vegetables, bread, soy beans, nuts and seeds, especially sesame.
Fluoride	Protects teeth against decay by making enamel more resistant.	In fish, and added to toothpaste. Some countries add it to water.
Iron	Needed to make red blood cells. Not enough iron can lead to anemia, which is particularly common among young girls.	Red meat, liver; beans (serve with fruit and vegetables or juice to aid absorption). Bread and cereals are often fortified with iron.
Iodine	Helps make thyroid hormones to keep cells and metabolism healthy.	Milk, sea fish, shellfish and other seafood, seaweed and iodized salt.
Magnesium	Numerous functions including helping turn food into energy.	Found in whole-grain cereals, nuts and green leafy vegetables.
Manganese	Numerous roles including helping to make and activate some of the enzymes in the body.	Contained in bread, nuts, cereals, green vegetables such as peas and beans and also in tea.
Phosphorus	Many roles including building strong bones and teeth.	Found in milk, cheese, meat, fish, rice, oats and eggs.
Potassium	Used to regulate body fluids and may help lower blood pressure.	Found in most foods. Fruit, vegetables and milk contain significant amounts.
Selenium	Helps immune system to function and acts as an antioxidant to protect cells (see page 21).	Found in meat, fish, cheese, eggs, cereal, bread and nuts, especially Brazil nuts.
Sodium	Regulation of both water content and nerve functioning.	Found in processed food and table salt. (See page 28 for more on sodium.)
Zinc	Essential for wound healing, growth and sexual development.	Found in milk, cheese, meat, eggs, fish, beans and whole-grain cereals.

What not to eat

Sugar, saturated fat and salt add flavor to food but are bad for children's health if they eat too much. It's best not to introduce too many salty, sugary and fatty foods in the first place, but if you do need to make changes to a child's diet, it's easier to do it in small steps. This section explains more about why children should be trying to cut down on certain foods and gives some ideas on how to go about it.

At a glance

Most children get more than enough salt from the food they eat, so you don't need to add more when cooking, or at the table.

Limit the amount of processed foods children eat, such as store-bought cookies, fast food, fried food and frozen dinners.

Try to avoid letting children eat trans-fats or too much saturated fat (see page 30). Use butter, margarine and mayonnaise sparingly.

Remove the fat from meat and the skin from chicken before you serve them.

Keep cakes, cookies and other sugary foods for parties and as treats.

To keep teeth healthy:

• Children should visit a dentist regularly.

• Any sugary foods and drinks should be limited to mealtimes as the saliva produced during eating helps dilute their harmful effects.

• Offer milk or water as main drinks. Try not to let children swill juice around their mouths. Drink carbonated drinks through a straw (or better not at all).

• Milk and cheese help strengthen teeth as their calcium and phosphate are absorbed in a process called remineralization.

The truth about sugar

There is no recommended 'safe' level of sugar consumption for children, but their average intake outstrips that of adults and it has been estimated that a child's risk of obesity increases by 60% for every extra sugar-sweetened drink they consume on a daily basis. As well as carbonated drinks, sugar is found in chips, canned foods, breakfast cereal, pre-packaged meals and many other foods. It may be listed as sugar, sucrose, glucose, dextrose, sorbitol or corn syrup. If these are one of the first few ingredients, the food is high in sugar. The sugar you buy in packages is almost pure sucrose.

What else is wrong with it?

The effect of sugar intake on children's behavior is hotly debated, but it's agreed that as blood sugar (the amount of glucose in the blood) levels fall, their bodies compensate by releasing the hormone adrenaline. The peak of this surge comes about four hours after eating sugar and may result in loss of concentration and erratic behavior. Sugary foods also often go hand in hand with fatty foods such as cakes and cookies and eating too many of these can lead to weight gain, especially if children are not getting enough exercise. The biggest problem with sugar, however, is that eating too much can lead to tooth decay. On the left are some ways to help children's teeth stay healthy.

Teeth should be brushed twice a day, with a fluoride toothpaste, but wait for an hour after eating to allow teeth to remineralize (see left).

Are some sugars better than others?

There are many different kinds of sugar substitutes on offer, and new ones are being developed all the time. There is a lot of debate about the safety of many of these, but essentially most nutritionists agree that refined sugar and sugar substitutes should be used in moderation.

Ways to cut down

The average can of cola contains nine teaspoons of sugar. Even low-calorie canned drinks are bad for teeth because they are acidic. Instead, you could try making carbonated drinks by mixing low-sugar fruit purees or juice concentrates with carbonated water. Here are some other ways to cut down on sugar:

• Opt for whole-grain, sugar-free cereal. Don't add sugar as milk contains a sugar called lactose.

• If children are used to sugar on cereal, wean them off it gradually by reducing the amount over several weeks.

• Honey is slightly less likely to cause tooth decay. Darker types have antioxidant properties too.

Real maple syrup has half the calories of sugar, is less likely to cause tooth decay, and contains small amounts of vitamins and minerals.

Safety point

NEVER give honey to children under the age of one, as it can cause infant botulism, a rare but very serious disease.

Cakes and cookies labeled 'low sugar' usually contain artificial sweeteners and may still be high in fat, so check labels (see page 34).

A pinch of salt?

Salt is a mineral and the human body needs a certain amount to function properly, but many children (and adults) have far too much in their diet. Bread, cereals, cookies, cakes and processed meat products such as bacon, sausage and ham are some of the main sources of salt. Processed foods account for the majority of salt in most people's diets.

Salt's chemical name is sodium chloride and it's the sodium in salt that can be harmful. Too much of it makes our bodies retain water and it is thought that this can lead to high blood pressure in later life (which can cause heart disease and strokes). Some processed foods contain other forms of sodium such as monosodium glutamate or baking soda, which some people are sensitive or have allergies to, so it's always worth reading labels carefully to check.

The small amounts of sodium found naturally in foods such as eggs, meat and fish account for about a fifth of all the salt we eat.

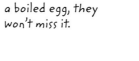

If children have never been offered salt with a boiled egg, they won't miss it.

How much salt?

It is recommended that preschool children should avoid added salt altogether and that children of school age have limited quantities. It's estimated that most children eat much more than is healthy, as it is in so many foods we eat. The best advice is to avoid giving children processed foods, like chips, cookies and cakes, and not add extra salt when cooking or at the table.

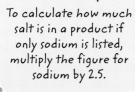

Useful tip

To calculate how much salt is in a product if only sodium is listed, multiply the figure for sodium by 2.5.

Salty foods

Below is a list of products that are often high in salt. You don't need to cut them out entirely, but it's a good idea to limit their intake. (Many manufacturers now offer low-salt options, so always read the label carefully.)

- anchovies
- bacon
- baked beans (canned)
- cookies
- breakfast cereals
- cheese
- chips
- French fries (if salt added)
- manufactured cooking sauces
- powdered gravy and sauce mixes
- hot-chocolate powder
- olives
- pickles
- crackers
- pizza
- pretzels
- ready-made meals and frozen dinners
- salted and dry roasted nuts
- dried meats (jerky)
- sausages
- smoked meat and fish
- soup (instant)
- soy sauce
- bouillon cubes
- canned spaghetti
- canned vegetables and beans (with added salt)

Useful tip
Ready-made sauces and broths often contain lots of salt. Instead, you could make a quantity of sauce and freeze it in batches to use when you need it.

Offer some lemon to squeeze on fish, rather than salt.

Cutting down

It is common practice to add salt to vegetables, pasta and other foods, and breaking this habit may make you worry that food is going to become tasteless. However, most food contains its own salt, and after a few weeks of not adding more during cooking or at the table, children may begin to taste the natural flavors of food better. Here are some other ways to add flavor and to cut down on salt.

Instead of salt, sprinkle dried or chopped fresh herbs on pasta, vegetables, meat and scrambled eggs.

- Check the salt content of packaged foods and choose items with reduced sodium.

- Make your own broth (page 72) and gravy (page 90), instead of using bouillon cubes.

- Try using different types of onions (brown, red, white, green onions, shallots) in cooking to add flavor.

- Use garlic, ginger, mild chili and lime in stir-fries.

- Roast vegetables such as red peppers, zucchini, potatoes, carrots and squash to bring out their flavor.

- If you have time, marinade meat and fish in advance to give them more flavor.

Good fats and bad fats

Fat is a source of energy and it helps the body to absorb vitamins A, D, E and K and to maintain healthy cells, but many children eat more 'bad' fats than they need. This can result in weight gain and, in the long term, heart disease. There are four types of fat: saturated, monounsaturated, polyunsaturated and trans-fat. All contain the same number of calories, but some should be avoided for other reasons.

Saturated fat

Saturated fat is the 'bad' fat that increases cholesterol, which can lead to health problems. It's usually solid at room temperature and comes mainly from meat or dairy products. Foods high in saturated fat include sausages, pies, cream, hard cheese and many cakes and cookies.

Palm and coconut oils also contain high levels of saturated fats. They are used by the food industry in cakes, cookies, chips, chocolates, French fries, cooking sauces and pastries. Look out for them on labels. (See page 34 for more about reading labels.)

Children need some fat in their diet to stay healthy, but try to make sure it's mainly the 'good' kind.

Trans-fats

Did you know?
Trans-fats are described on labels as 'hydrogenated' or 'partially hydrogenated' vegetable oils.

Trans-fats are also 'bad'. They are vegetable fats that have been solidified by a process called hydrogenation and are widely used in manufactured cakes, cookies, chips, fast food, cake mixes and pre-packaged meals. Trans-fats act like saturated fats and are thought to have no nutritional value. Some scientists also believe that children's brain chemistry is being altered by eating trans-fats.

Good fats

Monounsaturated fats are 'good' and are thought to help counterbalance the cholesterol levels of saturated fats and to prevent certain cancers. Polyunsaturated fat is also beneficial, especially Omega-3 fatty acids from fish (see page 19) and Omega-6 from some plant foods. 'Good' fat sources include:

• oily fish such as sardines, herring and mackerel
• soy, canola, sunflower and corn oils
• nuts and seeds and their oils
• olives and olive oil
• avocados

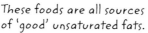

These foods are all sources of 'good' unsaturated fats.

Buying and storing oil

Cooking oils can become rancid when exposed to heat, light or air, so try to buy oils in dark brown or green containers and store them away from sunlight as this prevents them from going bad too quickly. Whenever possible, look for 'expeller-pressed' unrefined oils as this method extracts oil without the use of chemicals.

Useful tip

Spread only one slice of a sandwich with butter and cut it out altogether on toast when there's another topping. Most children won't notice the difference.

Butter and margarine

Butter contains saturated fats and cholesterol. While the saturated fats can raise cholesterol in the blood, the actual cholesterol in butter has been found to have little effect. Unless you choose a low-fat variety, margarine contains the same amount of fat as butter. Hard margarine is high in saturated fat and should be used sparingly. Soft margarine is generally trans-fat free and low in saturated fats. Margarine contains vitamin E and is fortified with vitamins A and D.

Butter should only be eaten in small quantities as it contains saturated fats.

Scientific analysis of food sold by major fast-food chains found that:

• Cheeseburgers contain more than a dozen added ingredients including acidity regulators, preservatives and emulsifiers.

• The potato in fries is mixed with partially hydrogenated vegetable oil (a trans-fat), dextrose and corn syrup (sugars), rice flour and salt.

• Grilled chicken breast is modified with a range of ingredients, including flour, starch, oil and lactose.

Making the treats for a birthday party yourself means you can keep an eye on ingredients.

Junk food

Junk food is food that has limited nutritional value. The term applies mainly to highly processed fast food such as burgers, pizzas and fries and to mass-produced pies, cakes and cookies. This kind of food contains high levels of sugar, fat, salt, colorings, preservatives and artificial flavorings.

Dangerous ingredients

Research into fast food suggests that sugary and fatty foods act like a drug and may be addictive. It seems that eating sugar and certain fats makes children overeat because they don't feel full, so the more junk they eat, the more their bodies crave it. After a junk food meal, there's a short-lived feeling of satisfaction, but they soon want to eat again.

Another worry about junk food is the way it is farmed before processing. Antibiotics are routinely used as growth-promoters in factory-farmed animals and hundreds of pesticides are licensed to protect crops against disease. Many enter the food chain and are still detectable in the junk food children eat. There are fears that, due to the way residues are stored in the human body, they may remain in fatty tissues for years, leading to possible immune system problems.

Bad mood food

Recent research indicates that diets high in processed foods deprive children's brains of essential nutrients required for mental well-being and development. This can lead to underachievement at school and a host of health problems. While children are getting bigger, they're not getting healthier. Some problems associated with a poor diet are:

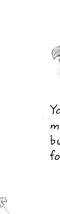

- constipation
- stomachaches
- excess weight gain
- tiredness
- lack of motivation

- learning difficulties
- irritability
- poor concentration
- depression
- anxiety

You can find out how to make your own healthy burgers and other 'fast' foods on pages 98 and 99.

What children eat can have an effect on their mood and behavior.

Useful tip

Oily fish, fresh fruit and vegetables, whole grains and nuts are all 'good mood' foods.

Ban the junk?

Junk food can be eaten occasionally, but really shouldn't be a regular part of children's diets and it's worth taking the time to explain why. Some of the information may go over their heads at first, but children like to be told the truth. The more you tell them, the more they'll absorb the facts.

The junk food industry has begun to make some changes in response to the bad press generated by research findings. Salads and sandwiches are now on many menus, alongside the burgers and fries, but their dressings and sauces may still contain harmful trans-fats, preservatives and so on.

Did you know?

A fast-food artificial strawberry flavored milk shake may contain over 50 different chemical 'ingredients' to achieve its 'natural' taste.

Food labeling

Food labels are packed with information, but the different terms and symbols can be confusing. There are rules that food manufacturers must follow that protect consumers from false claims or misleading descriptions and clear guidelines on what labels can and can't show.

Serving sizes and servings per container must be listed on the container.

The energy value of the food is shown as calories and calories from fat.

The amounts of protein, carbohydrates and fats are given in grams (g). This makes it easy to check if foods are fatty or high in sugar, for example.

If a food claims to be high in fiber or low in fat, salt or sugar etc., it must meet strict government definitions in order to make the claim.

The amount of vitamins and minerals in a food are given as a percentage of the Recommended Daily Value (RDV), which has been determined by nutritionists.

Percent Daily Values are based on a 2,000-calorie diet. Your child's daily values will be higher or lower depending on calorie needs.

Organic food needs to be approved by a certified organization whose logo is shown. Organic food cannot be genetically modified or have been irradiated.

Products containing milk, eggs, nuts, fish, shellfish, soy, wheat, celery, mustard, sesame and sulfur dioxide are often labeled as they are common allergens.

Manufacturers are obligated by law to give nutritional information.

Labels must include total calories, calories from fat, total fat, saturated fat, cholesterol, sodium, total carbohydrates, dietary fiber, sugars, protein, Vitamin A, Vitamin C, calcium and iron.

All ingredients must be shown in order of weight, so if sugar is first, the product has a high sugar content. You can look for things you may want to avoid.

NUTRITION FACTS

Serving Size: 8 crackers (31g)

Servings Per Container: About 13

ALLERGY WARNING: Contains wheat and soy products.

Amount Per Serving:

Calories 130   Calories from Fat 25

	% Daily Value*
Total Fat 3g	5%
Saturated Fat 0.5g	3%
Trans Fat 0g	
Polyunsaturated Fat 1.5g	
Monounsaturated Fat 0.5g	
Cholesterol 0mg	0%
Sodium 190mg	8%
Potassium 40mg	1%
Total Carbohydrate 24g	8%
Dietary Fiber 1g	4%
Sugars 8g	
Protein 2g	

Vitamin A 0%	·	Vitamin C 0%	
Calcium 0%	·	Iron 6%	

* Percent Daily Values are based on a 2,000-calorie diet. Your daily values may be higher or lower depending on your calorie needs:

	Calories:	2,000	2,500
Total Fat	Less than	65g	80g
Sat Fat	Less than	20g	25g
Cholesterol	Less than	300mg	300mg
Sodium	Less than	2,400mg	2,400mg
Potassium		3,500mg	3,500mg
Total Carbohydrate		300g	375g
Dietary Fiber		25g	30g

INGREDIENTS: ENRICHED FLOUR (WHEAT FLOUR, NIACIN, REDUCED IRON, THIAMINE MONONITRATE {VITAMIN B1}, RIBOFLAVIN {VITAMIN B2}, FOLIC ACID), SOYBEAN OIL AND/OR PARTIALLY HYDROGENATED COTTONSEED OIL, HIGH FRUCTOSE CORN SYRUP, HONEY, LEAVENING (BAKING SODA AND/OR CALCIUM PHOSPHATE), SALT, ARTIFICIAL FLAVOR, SOY LECITHIN - AN EMULSIFER, CORNSTARCH.

Special diets and exercise

In this section there is advice on how to make sure young vegetarians stay healthy. There's also information on food allergies and how to recognize symptoms, along with ways to prevent or to counteract excessive weight gain in children through diet and exercise.

At a glance

A vegetarian diet, like others, needs to be balanced. Only non-dairy eating vegetarians may need supplements.

Children often grow out of food allergies.

Allergic reactions range from those causing mild discomfort to ones that require urgent medical attention.

A healthy diet is low in fat, salt and sugar and high in fruit, vegetables, low-fat dairy and whole-grain foods.

Try to limit the time children spend on sedentary activities such as watching TV and playing computer games to two hours or less a day.

An hour's exercise a day is recommended and this can be broken down into 10-minute chunks.

A vegetarian diet

Some children now choose to become vegetarian and their diet, like any other, requires some planning and attention to what they eat. Vegetarians don't eat any meat, but most do still eat dairy products and perhaps fish. Vegetarian diets are very healthy if you make sure children get all the nutrients they need in the ways suggested on these pages.

Vegetarian diets need to be well balanced.

It's especially important to make sure vegetarian children are getting enough:

• calcium
• protein
• iron
• zinc
• vitamin B12

Make sure vegetarians:

• Eat fruit or drink fruit juice with meals — their vitamin C helps improve iron absorption.

• Eat grains and proteins in combination so that they get enough essential amino acids (see right).

Like other children, young vegetarians should also:

• Eat three servings of dairy products each day.

• Eat at least five servings of fruit and vegetables a day.

• Keep active and get a good dose of vitamin D a day by getting outside in the sun (with sunscreen on).

Protein combinations

Protein is made of amino acids, some of which are known as 'essential amino acids' because the body can't make them itself. It's important to get some of each of these at the same time, but only meat, fish and eggs contain the complete mix. Vegetarians can get essential amino acids by eating grains and proteins in combinations, such as:

• baked beans on toast
• lentil soup and bread
• bread and cheese
• peanut butter sandwich
• rice and dhal
• hummus and pita bread

Calcium sources

Recent studies have found that modern diets often contain only a third of the calcium needed to maintain healthy bones and teeth. Calcium is obtainable from:

• eggs
• tofu
• green leafy vegetables
• whole-grain bread
• sardines and salmon
• walnuts, Brazil nuts, almonds, pecans and cashews
• dairy foods such as cheese, yogurt and milk
• pumpkin, sunflower and sesame seeds

All of these foods are sources of calcium.

Iron, zinc and vitamin B12

A lack of iron causes tiredness, which can result in learning and behavioral problems in children. Although meat is the richest source, iron can also be found in:

- whole-grain bread, rice and cereals
- almonds, walnuts and peanuts
- prunes and dried apricots
- green leafy vegetables

- beans and lentils
- shellfish
- olives
- eggs

Green leafy vegetables provide iron and calcium.

Zinc is vital for the immune system. It is found in meat, eggs, milk and shellfish and also obtained by plants from soil. Non-meat eaters can get enough zinc in their diets by eating a range of foods that contain zinc:

- freshly popped popcorn
- sunflower and sesame seeds
- almonds, Brazil nuts, peanuts, walnuts
- whole-wheat bread and pasta

- carrots and turnips
- lobster and crab
- garlic
- eggs

Useful tip

For a dose of vitamins and minerals, provide nuts, seeds and dried fruit for children to snack on during low-energy times such as mid-afternoon.

Vitamin B12 occurs naturally in animal products but not in plant foods and lack of it can cause anemia and nerve damage, so non-dairy eating vegetarians may need to take B12 supplements. B12 is found in:

- brie, cheddar, Edam, mozzarella and cottage cheese
- trout, haddock and halibut

- sardines, tuna and salmon
- fortified cereals
- eggs

Falafel (page 99) with whole-wheat pita bread, salad and tzatziki (page 68) is a well-balanced vegetarian meal.

Food allergies and intolerance

Research indicates that allergies are on the increase and that as many as eight percent of children will suffer from some kind of allergy. The good news is that most will grow out of it. Food allergies are often hereditary and most reactions are mild. Some, however, in a minority of cases, require urgent medical treatment. The most common reactions are to milk, nuts, eggs, soy, shellfish and wheat. You can find out more about these allergies on pages 120 and 121.

Even everyday foods such as eggs, wheat and nuts can trigger allergic reactions in some children.

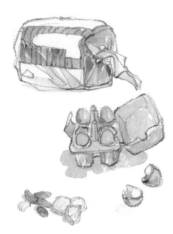

Allergic or intolerant?

Food allergies and food intolerance are types of food sensitivity. An allergic reaction is when the immune system reacts against a particular food and it can be life threatening. Food intolerance doesn't involve the immune system but can make the sufferer feel very sick and affect long-term health. Symptoms of allergic reactions (listed on the left) can vary and may be more or less severe on different occasions and they may appear within minutes or up to several hours after eating.

Symptoms of a reaction:

- *Wheezing and shortness of breath*
- *Swelling of lips and throat*
- *Runny or blocked nose*
- *Coughing*
- *Dry, itchy throat and tongue*
- *Itchy skin or rash*
- *Nausea and feeling bloated*
- *Stomach cramps*
- *Diarrhea and/or vomiting*
- *Sore, red and itchy eyes*

Tell all children not to share the contents of their lunch boxes.

Safety point

If you are feeding other people's children, always find out if they have any allergies beforehand.

Oral allergy syndrome

Certain foods, particularly fruits and vegetables, can cause itching or rashes when they touch the lips and mouth. These reactions usually happen to hay-fever sufferers, as the allergens are found in pollen as well as some fruit and vegetables. Cooking often destroys them, so even if a child can't eat raw apples, they may be able to eat them cooked.

Some kinds of fresh fruit can trigger oral allergy syndrome in some children.

Checking the label

Manufacturers must list foods that commonly cause allergic reactions on the label. Some say 'may contain nuts' or 'may contain seeds'. This means that even though nuts or seeds aren't deliberately included, the manufacturer can't guarantee that the product doesn't contain small amounts of them. It's important to avoid these products if a child has a nut or seed allergy.

Labels on packaging are becoming more informative about what foods may contain.

Safety point

Seek urgent medical help for any symptoms of what is known as an anaphylactic reaction. They may occur in different parts of the body at the same time and include:

• Rashes
• Swelling of lips and throat
• Difficulty breathing
• A rapid fall in blood pressure and loss of consciousness

Children who have an allergy that may provoke such a reaction need to carry adrenaline around in the form of a pen, called an epinephrine, which can be easily administered.

Eating a balanced diet

Being unable to eat certain foods will not harm children's health. It is the overall balance of the diet that matters. If you are concerned about a child's diet, it's a good idea to talk to a dietician, who will be able to advise you.

Staying a healthy weight

Since the 1970s children have become taller but also overweight and an increasing number are becoming obese. Children are described as obese when their weight could seriously damage their health, and doctors are seeing more overweight children developing type 2 diabetes. Excessive weight gain in an otherwise healthy child is caused by a combination of eating too many calories and not being active enough.

Studies have found three main reasons for the increase in child obesity:

• Greater reliance on cars and decline in walking on a daily basis (especially walking to school).

• Rapid expansion of the fast-food industry and the resulting high consumption of calories.

• An increase in television watching and playing computer games rather than physical activity.

Games that get children moving should be part of their daily routine.

Changing lifestyles and diets

To maintain a healthy weight, children need a diet that is:

• Low in sugar
• Low in salt
• Low in fat (particularly saturated fat)
• High in fruit and vegetables (at least five servings a day)
• High in starchy carbohydrate foods, such as bread, rice and pasta – particularly whole grains.

Long before mass processing methods, our ancestors had to expend a lot of energy hunting, gathering and farming. Scientists believe that children's (and adults') bodies are still programmed to crave the high-energy foods needed for this way of life. Now many people are far less active, and these foods provide more energy than their bodies can use. The surplus energy is turned into fat. To maintain a healthy weight, children need a balanced diet, low in fat and sugar and with plenty of grains, fruit and vegetables.

Chubby or overweight?

Small children often have rounded stomachs that flatten as they grow, but overweight children have rolls of fat on their bellies and it's this that worries health professionals. Overweight and obese children were once just chubby children, so watch out for children in these early stages and help them toward sensible eating and activity as a part of their daily routine. There are some ideas to help on the right.

• Try to stick to a meal routine and try for an hour of activity every day.

• Keep servings moderate in size and encourage children to eat slowly.

• Give children a healthy snack if they're not going to eat for a while.

• Keep a careful eye on the fat and sugar content of foods by checking labels.

• Provide water or low-fat milk rather than soda or other sweetened drinks.

Low GI foods

Dieticians recommend following a low GI (Glycemic Index) diet. Foods with a low GI value release sugar into the blood slowly, providing a steady supply of energy and leaving the body feeling full for longer. These are some low GI foods:

• pearl barley
• red lentils
• chickpeas
• butter beans
• whole-grain spaghetti
• bran cereal
• old-fashioned oatmeal
• corn
• roasted peanuts
• whole-grain bread
• baked beans in tomato sauce

• low-fat yogurt
• dried apricots
• cherries
• grapefruit
• apples
• pears
• bananas
• milk

Chickpeas, butter beans and other beans are convenient low GI foods.

Feeling full

Several studies have shown that eating foods such as soups or salads at the start of a meal also creates a feeling of fullness and reduces the amount of food eaten overall. Other studies have found that even small reductions in energy-dense (high calorie) foods and serving sizes result in lower levels of energy intake and fewer calories.

Useful tip

Remember that removing sweets from a child's daily diet isn't punishment. You're doing them a big favor by not allowing them to become dependent on unhealthy foods.

Children and exercise

Exercise has the benefit not only of controlling weight but also of promoting overall physical health and it is recommended that children should have at least an hour a day. Establishing exercise as part of a daily routine will be of huge benefit as children become adults and help combat health problems including heart disease and osteoporosis.

Play is the best form of exercise for young children.

Did you know?

Active children have fewer chronic health problems, are less likely to become obese and are more able to tackle daily challenges.

The many benefits

Exercise also has a positive effect on children's moods and can help raise their self-esteem. Sports scientists have found evidence of a chemical produced during exercise called phenyl ethylamine, which raises blood pressure and blood sugar levels, resulting in a sense of well-being. Sports help mental agility too. Children develop all kinds of skills including strategy, negotiation, thinking ahead, working with others, balance and coordination.

Exercise builds up muscle mass and strength and provides an increased ability to burn fat both at rest and at play. Weight-bearing activities such as running and gymnastics also help to increase bone density, which helps maintain bone health in later life and protect against osteoporosis.

Set a good example

As a parent or caregiver, you can set a good example by being active yourself, for instance by walking to the second nearest stop to take the bus. Racing children up the stairs (instead of taking the elevator) shows them that being out of breath can be fun.

Useful tip

If you are close enough to school, consider organizing a 'walking bus' or 'cycling bus' where parents take turns gathering children and escorting them to school instead of driving.

Most children enjoy learning to ride a bike, and cycling is very good exercise.

Studies have found that four to seven year-old children who have active mothers are twice as likely to be active compared with those who have inactive mothers, and if their fathers are active too, they are even more likely to be so themselves. To motivate children to include activity as part of their daily routine, stress play rather than exercise, and promote activities you and your child enjoy. Remember that regular exercise:

- Reduces body fat.
- Strengthens bones.
- Aids coordination, balance and flexibility.
- Fights depression and anxiety.
- Gives us more energy.
- Improves stamina.
- Makes us feel happier.

Limit screen time

Children are naturally active, but the computer and TV can lure them into lethargy, so health advisers suggest 'screen time' should be limited to two hours a day. Pulling children away from the TV and computer can be an ordeal, but active children really are happier.

More exercise ideas

An hour of activity a day may sound like an impossibility, but it doesn't have to be done all at once and most children do at least half an hour's activity at school. It's when they get home and on weekends that you need to stop them from sinking too far into the sofa.

Ten minutes at a time

Breaking the hour up into ten-minute chunks is fine. You could, for example, try getting everyone to jump rope for ten minutes as part of the daily routine. You'll need to increase this gradually, as it takes a while to build stamina. To stop it from getting boring, jump to music and vary the actions by skipping backward, hopping from one foot to another and crossing your arms as you jump. You could also set other challenges, such as hopping while bouncing a ball on a racquet. These are some other activities to try:

Ideas for inside activities:

• Put on some music and dance around.

• Buy some plastic hoops and try hula-hooping.

• Try a game of balloon volleyball.

• Get children to help with the housework.

- cycling
- swimming
- skating
- soccer
- trampolining
- ball games

- kite flying
- dancing
- digging
- raking leaves
- playing catch
- chasing games

- gymnastics
- volleyball
- fast walking
- climbing
- sledding

Safety points

Children should wear helmets for cycling and also knee and elbow pads for roller-skating and skateboarding.

If they walk or cycle to school, or play outdoors, make sure they're aware of road safety, and the importance of staying in a group.

Once children learn some basic ball skills, they find it hard to resist practicing them.

Fun with food

Getting children involved in grocery shopping and in the planning and preparation of meals can encourage them to think about where their food comes from, to be more aware of what they're eating and to try new foods. Helping in the kitchen and growing food, even if it's just a few herbs on a windowsill, are things most children enjoy, and it's worth taking a little time to teach them a few basic skills.

At a glance

Most children enjoy helping in the kitchen and become more adventurous if they are involved in making meals.

Planning meals a week at a time helps ensure you are giving children a balanced diet.

Providing healthy snacks is a useful way to make sure children are eating the right kinds of foods.

Growing your own food can be a good way to get children more interested in what they eat.

It may take up to ten attempts to get a child to accept a new food, so keep trying.

Children in the kitchen

Learning to cook provides children with a range of useful skills that they can build on as they get older. Cooking sessions are also a good time to talk about different kinds of food, and about healthy eating, but before you start, it's important to establish a few rules of safety and hygiene. To maintain children's interest, you need to decide which jobs they are capable of doing; while younger children may be happy mixing and mashing, older children need more challenging tasks, such as cracking eggs and measuring ingredients.

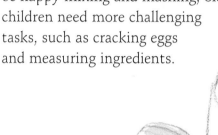

• Everyone should wash their hands before starting to cook.

• Wash all fruit and vegetables before cooking or eating.

• You should use separate boards for meat and fish, and fruit and vegetables.

• Always wash hands after handling raw meat or fish.

• Check use-by dates on ingredients before you use them.

Young children can roll out dough, but you need to do the cutting.

What can they do?

There are plenty of jobs that even young children can do in the kitchen, but only you can judge when a child is ready to learn to use a knife, stir a hot sauce or open the oven door. It is essential, however, that you keep a very close eye on children at all times in the kitchen, whatever they are doing and however experienced they are. These are some basic skills that most children can learn easily:

• Using a sieve
• Kneading dough
• Chopping vegetables
• Cracking eggs
• Whisking egg whites

• Rolling and cutting out dough
• Stirring and mixing butter and flour
• Squeezing citrus fruit
• Peeling vegetables with a peeler
• Mashing potatoes with a masher

Food safety

Remember the rules of food safety when storing and cooking food: store cooked and raw food separately and use separate utensils for raw and cooked meat. Don't leave food out of the refrigerator for more than two hours and store raw meat covered, on a plate, on the bottom shelf of the refrigerator where it can't touch other foods.

Don't put ready-to-eat food, such as salad, on a worktop that has been touched by raw meat, unless you have cleaned it thoroughly first. Always make sure food is cooked all the way through before serving, store any leftovers in the refrigerator promptly and eat them within five days.

Making it easier

There are some pieces of equipment you can buy that make things easier for children in the kitchen. Rubber mats stop bowls from moving around when they are mixing. Utensils with chunky handles and mini rolling pins are easier for small hands to grip. Chopping boards with raised edges stop things from falling on the floor.

Some child-friendly utensils, such as a small mixing bowl and a mini rolling pin make cooking easier for small children.

Kitchen safety:

• Don't run in the kitchen.

• Don't touch electric equipment with wet hands.

• Stand back when you open the oven door and use oven gloves to handle hot things.

• Have a clear space on a heatproof surface ready to put hot pans and dishes on.

• Turn pan handles away from you on the stove and don't leave utensils in hot pans.

• Be cautious when frying, as hot fat can splatter, and be careful of steam from pans.

• Wash any sharp knives especially carefully.

Useful tip

Don't forget to tie back long hair, roll up long sleeves and put on an apron for cooking.

Buying fruit and vegetables when in season is an easy way to keep the menu changing.

Useful tip
Remember whole-grain varieties are healthiest because they are higher in fiber and contain more nutrients.

Planning meals

If you can, planning what you're going to eat a week ahead makes shopping and cooking easier. By drawing up a menu, you can make sure that children are getting a balanced diet and also try to include meals everyone enjoys.

Meals should be planned around carbohydrates. Don't forget that at least half of all 'grains' should be whole grains. Besides rice, pasta and potatoes, don't forget things like tortilla wraps (see page 67) or other grains such as couscous (recipe on page 84). Most children do not get enough vegetables, so try to include a variety at each meal.

Protein

Although protein should only be about a tenth of what's on the plate, it's still a key element and particularly important for children's growth. In a week, children should be eating at least one, and ideally two, servings of oily fish. Otherwise, remember to include small quantities of high-quality lean meat (or a vegetarian substitute) and a few meat-free meals per week.

Buy foods you know your children will eat, but also some new ones to try.

Choosing meals

Try to get children involved in meal planning as well as cooking. They could help write (or draw) shopping lists or make a list of their favorite meals and put them on a chart that covers a week or two. You could talk to them about including something like rice, pasta or bread and at least two vegetables with each meal, and see what they come up with. Cooking a double quantity and freezing half for another time could be worth the effort for foods you eat regularly. Soup, pasta sauce and pizza dough all freeze well, for example.

Children could help you write shopping lists based on the meals they have chosen.

Children could add stickers or comments to their chart to show which meals they enjoyed most.

In grocery stores children can look for the 'traffic lights' labeling system that some food producers now use.

Sugar 2.7g per serving	LOW
Fat 20g per serving	MEDIUM
Salt 3.8g per serving	HIGH

A range of colors

Different colored fruit and vegetables contain different vitamins, minerals and antioxidants (see page 21). Red, orange and yellow foods contain different nutrients than green foods and they complement each other, working together to keep the body's immune system running well. If children eat fruits and vegetables of all the different colors of the rainbow, along with whole grains, nuts, seeds and beans, they will be getting a full range of essential nutrients. They could keep a record of the colors they eat and try for the whole range.

Traffic light label

Healthy snacking

Despite the conventional wisdom of not eating between meals, many studies have shown that it is more sensible for young children to eat lots of small meals throughout the day instead of the customary three big ones.

The sensation of hunger is caused by low sugar levels in the blood and dips in energy. By keeping the body stoked up with nutrients by means of small snacks, the energy is released evenly. However, snacks for children shouldn't mean chips, sugary cookies and candy bars that may lead to erratic behavior and spoiled appetites. There are plenty of healthy snacks that can keep hunger pangs at bay until the next meal.

When you're going on a long journey, pack a picnic to avoid having to buy unhealthy snacks.

Children are often very hungry when they come home from school. Put out a bowl of nuts, seeds and dried fruit for them.

Whole-wheat toast, muffins or bagels may be popular.

Children are better tempered when their energy levels are kept topped up with healthy snacks.

Getting a balance

Healthy snacking is a good way of making sure children eat at least five servings of fruit and vegetables a day as well as some of the other foods that are good for them such as nuts, whole-wheat bread and small amounts of low-fat cheese. It doesn't really matter if their appetites are reduced at mealtimes, as long as what they eat fits into the overall balance of foods that should be eaten every day.

Useful tip

A fruit smoothie provides a vitamin boost, a serving of dairy and counts toward five-a-day. See page 63 for a recipe to try.

Whole-wheat raspberry muffins are a healthy treat (recipe on page 59).

Are treats allowed?

Treats can be part of a healthy diet but they should be treats – something for special occasions. Like adults, children deprived of something can binge when they finally get access to it, so moderation is the key. You may find it's easier not to have unhealthy foods in the house most of the time, because if children know there are cookies, they'll want cookies and not the food you offer them.

As much as possible, try to set a good example, too. Don't tell children that chocolate is bad for them, for instance, then eat lots yourself. Show that you enjoy healthy food and try to sit down to eat meals together as often as you can.

You could offer whole-grain pita bread and raw vegetables with dips such as hummus, tzatziki or guacamole (recipes on pages 68–89) as a snack.

Strips of pita bread

Carrot and celery sticks

More healthy snack ideas:

- A small bag of corn chips with salsa dip
- A plain rice cake, or topped with peanut butter
- Half an avocado with some low-fat cottage cheese
- Dried fruit with (for over fives only) a few nuts
- Whole-wheat crackers with cottage cheese or hummus
- Cheese cubes with grapes
- Frozen yogurt
- A frozen chunk of banana or peeled orange on a stick
- Dried or fresh fruit with cottage cheese
- A yogurt topped with flaked coconut or dried apricots
- Thin strips of ham wrapped around prunes
- Whole-grain bagel with low-fat cream cheese
- Mini rice cakes and a small piece of cheese

Growing your own food

Whether you've got a garden, deck, balcony or windowsill, there is plenty that you can grow. Planting seeds and watching them grow and produce food can be an eye-opener for children and may also be an incentive for them to try fruits and vegetables they might otherwise reject.

Herbs are among the easiest plants to grow and can be used in a variety of ways:

• Rosemary, sage and bay leaf add flavor when roasted with potatoes and other vegetables.

• Parsley is rich in iron and vitamin C and can be sprinkled over many foods.

• Cilantro grows quickly from seed in windowsill pots and works well with stir-fries (see page 100).

Sunflower seeds

Sunflower seeds are easy to grow and can be planted in pots on a windowsill and then transferred to larger pots, or a garden when the seedlings are 4 inches high. You can harvest the seeds from your sunflowers when the petals have lost their color. You need to remove the shells before you eat them.

Each sunflower has about 2,000 seeds, which can be added to granola, crumbles, bread and salads.

Strawberries in pots

Make sure any plants you grow in pots, such as strawberries, are kept well watered.

Strawberries need to be kept off the soil, so growing them in pots is a good idea. Use a multi-purpose compost and put a layer of stones on the top, so, when watering, the soil is not splashed onto the fruits. Once the berries start to develop, and turn red, they need to be protected from birds. The plants are tough and can survive outside all year.

Tomatoes and potatoes

You could grow some tomato plants from seeds in early spring or buy a couple in late spring and keep them on an indoor windowsill until any danger of frost has passed. Gradually get them used to the outdoors by bringing them out during the day. Plant them out in a basket, pot of compost or in the ground and water frequently, which may mean twice a day when it's hot. Feed them with a tomato feed, according to the instructions on the package.

Put five chitted (sprouted) potatoes in a large plastic bucket with drainage holes in the bottom on 4 inches of compost. As the shoots begin to grow, gradually add more compost until the container is full. Dig up the potatoes as soon as the leaves turn yellow. Potatoes can be grown from early spring and will be ready by summer.

Place a few stones in pots, to help with drainage, then add compost on top.

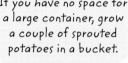

Useful tip
If you have no space for a large container, grow a couple of sprouted potatoes in a bucket.

Sprouting seeds and salads

Sprouting seeds increases their vitamin and protein content, and they can be added to salads and stir-fries. You could try sprouting chickpeas, mung beans and lentils. Soak the seeds overnight, then drain and place in a bowl with a plate on top. Wash and drain every day and they should be ready to eat in four to five days.

Salad leaves can be ready to eat within a month of planting. Their seeds are tiny, so it's best to sow a few in a seed tray and plant out stronger seedlings in a growing bag or pot after about ten days.

Children may be more willing to try different kinds of salad leaves if they have grown them from seeds.

- Don't let children snack for at least an hour before meals.

- Give children lots of praise when they eat a new food.

- Experiment with new foods and flavors yourself.

- Talk about flavors and textures — sweet, salty, crunchy, chewy, and so on.

- Let children choose a new fruit or vegetable to try when they go shopping with you.

Introducing new foods

Encouraging children to try new foods is another key to building a healthy diet. Research shows that children start to develop their adult food preferences around the age of five, so having a taste for a variety of foods at an early age can positively influence their long-term health prospects.

Count to ten

Research also shows that it can take up to ten tries for a new food to be accepted. Encourage children to try something new by letting them know how much you like it. Offering a rejected food in a new place may work, so try it again on vacation or when visiting friends. Remember to try introducing a new vegetable by mixing it with a food that they already like, by hiding it in a sauce, or with a little grated cheese on it.

Try introducing a new food in lunch boxes. If children are hungry, they may try it.

Peer pressure sometimes works, so seeing a friend eating a rejected food may encourage a child to try it again.

Useful tip

Pizza, pasta and wraps offer opportunities to try out new flavors. Let children make their own by putting out bowls of toppings for them to try.

Don't worry

A lot of anxiety can build up around food and meals, especially if, despite your efforts, children are 'picky eaters'. However frustrating this is, it's important not to appear too concerned about what does and doesn't get eaten, and to avoid power struggles over food. However, if you are truly worried about a child's diet and think it might be affecting their health and development, consult the child's doctor.

Breakfast ideas

After a night's sleep, children's bodies and brains need fuel to get going properly. The kinds of food they eat at breakfast can set the mood for the rest of the day, influencing their physical and mental performance. This section gives some ideas for breakfasts for days when everyone needs to get out the door early, and others for when there is a little more time.

At a glance

Research shows that missing breakfast leads to higher cholesterol and lower insulin levels, which are both risk factors for heart disease in the long term.

Children's breakfasts should include fruit, fiber, calcium, and carbohydrates.

Base everyday breakfasts on whole-grain cereals or whole-grain bread and offer milk, juice or a smoothie to drink.

Stop breakfasts from becoming predictable by varying what you provide, especially on days when you have more time.

Cereal bars may look healthy, but often contain lots of sugar and saturated fat.

• Some cereals contain a lot of salt and sugar, so check labels carefully.

• Use low-fat milk (for children over two) to keep breakfast low in fat.

• Add some fruit or berries to the bowl. (See the ideas on page 62.)

Breakfast cereals

The carbohydrates in breakfast cereals provide energy to help children get going in the morning. A sugar-free whole-grain cereal, sugar-free muesli, granola or oatmeal are all healthy choices. A bowl of one of these with milk, together with a glass of juice or some fruit will give children a head start on their daily requirements of vitamins, minerals, fiber and five-a-day while also providing enough energy to keep them going until lunch.

Bananas release energy slowly so are a useful breakfast food. Try adding a few slices to a bowl of cereal.

Oatmeal

Ingredients for Oatmeal (serves 2)

• 3 oz. rolled oats (old-fashioned oatmeal)
• 1 cup milk
• a little honey

Avoid instant oatmeal, as it contains a lot of added sugar.

When the weather is cold, you could provide oatmeal. A recent study found that children who ate oatmeal for breakfast were less likely to feel hungry between meals and also ate less at lunchtime, so it is a good breakfast for children who need to lose weight, at any time of year.

1. Pour the rolled oats and milk into a non-stick saucepan over medium heat.
2. Bring to a boil, stirring regularly, and then simmer for about 5–7 minutes, or until the oatmeal has thickened and cooked through (taste it to test). If the mixture becomes too thick, add extra milk or some water.
3. Leave to cool for a while before serving, and let children stir in honey or maple syrup if they like.

Granola

Ingredients for Granola (4 servings)

- 2 tablespoons whole hazelnuts
- 1 tablespoon canola oil
- 3 tablespoons honey
- 15 tablespoons or ²/₃ cup (5 oz.) rolled oats (old-fashioned oatmeal)
- 3 tablespoons sunflower seeds
- 1 tablespoon sesame seeds
- 3 tablespoons dried apricots (chopped)
- 2 tablespoons raisins

This crunchy homemade cereal can be served immediately with milk and fruit or stored in an airtight container to use later, so make a larger quantity if you want to keep some.

1. Preheat the oven to 350°F. Put the hazelnuts in a clean plastic food bag and close the end. Roll a rolling pin over the nuts to crush them.
2. Pour the canola oil and honey into a pan. Stir them together over low heat until the mixture is warm and runny, then remove from the heat.
3. Add the hazelnuts, oats, and all the seeds to the pan. Stir until all the ingredients are well coated.
4. Pour the mixture onto a baking tray, use a spoon to spread it out evenly and bake in the oven for 15 minutes, until it turns golden.
5. Leave the granola on the tray for 5 minutes to cool.
6. Pour into a large bowl, break into small clusters, and stir in the apricot pieces and raisins before serving or storing.

Seeds are rich in protein, minerals and vitamins E and B.

Granola can be served with fresh fruit and milk or yogurt.

Bread for breakfast

A couple of slices of whole-wheat toast spread lightly with jam provide children with the energy from starchy carbohydrates that they need first thing in the morning. Spreads such as peanut butter are good too, but make sure you buy a low-salt product.

You could also try serving cheese on toast for breakfast. Grate a small chunk of cheese and scatter it over lightly toasted bread and then grill until the cheese has melted. Peanut butter and cheese contain high levels of protein so are useful sources for children who don't eat fish or meat.

Useful tip

Some jellies and jams contain very little fruit. Look for those with a high fruit content, such as fruit preserves.

Encourage children to spread butter or jam thinly on their toast.

Adding tomato slices to cheese on toast counts toward a child's five-a-day.

Bagels

• Serve bagels with low-fat cream cheese and tomato.

• Try with smoked trout or a fish paté (see page 75).

• Try scrambled egg on its own or with chopped chives.

These soft bread rings are a Jewish breakfast speciality. They are the only bread that is boiled before it is baked and this gives the bagels a chewy texture that many children like. Bagels are low in fat too. Buy whole-grain if you can and serve them sliced in half, lightly toasted. Savory bagels are traditionally eaten with cream cheese and smoked salmon, but there are many other variations you could try, such as those on the left.

Fruity breads

Fruit can help to make breads and buns taste sweeter and more 'interesting' for children. Try serving bagels, fruit loaves, whole-grain waffles, English muffins or French toast for breakfast. These foods provide energy from carbohydrates, and the dried fruit content helps boost vitamin intake and counts toward five-a-day.

French toast (see page 61) with raisins or other fruit added

Serve English muffins cut in half and lightly toasted with jam or peanut butter.

Toasted fruit bread makes a satisfying breakfast for hungry children.

Mini berry muffins

This makes about 36 mini muffins and you can use raspberries, blueberries or blackberries. The mashed bananas replace some of the sugar you would usually add to muffins and makes them healthier. You could put some in the freezer as they defrost quickly for a breakfast treat.

Ingredients for Mini berry muffins

- ½ cup butter (softened)
- ¼ cup soft brown sugar
- 2 ripe bananas (mashed)
- 2 eggs
- ½ cup milk
- 1 ¾ cups whole-wheat flour
- 3 teaspoons baking powder
- ½ cup rolled oats
- 1 cup (10 oz.) berries

There is a photograph of these muffins made with raspberries on page 51.

1. Preheat the oven to 350°F.
2. Line a mini muffin tray with paper baking cups.
3. Cream the butter and sugar until light and fluffy.
4. Stir in the bananas, eggs, milk, flour, baking powder and rolled oats. Mix together well.
5. Gently fold in the berries.
6. Spoon into the baking cups and bake in the oven for 12–15 minutes, or until golden brown.
7. Leave to cool on a wire rack before serving or freezing.

Eggs

There are various ways to cook eggs and combine them with carbohydrates for healthy, everyday breakfasts. Eggs are high in protein and contain a range of vitamins.

Scrambling and boiling

Scrambled eggs are simply beaten eggs poured into a pan containing a teaspoon of melted butter or olive oil and cooked to your child's preferred consistency. Try not to overcook the scrambled egg mixture, or it will become rubbery. Beating in a little milk will make the eggs fluffier.

For hard-boiled eggs, gently drop the eggs, whole, into a saucepan of boiling water and let them cook for 7–10 minutes.

Serve boiled eggs with thinly buttered toast cut into strips.

Useful tip

For poached eggs, make sure you use really fresh eggs. Crack them into a pan of simmering water and cook for 4 minutes.

Scrambled eggs go well with lightly toasted English muffins or toast.

One-egg omelet

Ingredients for One-egg omelet (serves 1)

• 1 teaspoon butter or olive oil
• 1 egg (beaten)

1. Melt the butter in a small frying pan, pour in the beaten egg and tilt the pan to spread it out.
2. Cook until the edges start to solidify.
3. Gently lift around the edges with a wooden spatula.
4. Fold one half over the other and serve immediately.

Spanish Omelet

This makes a filling and substantial breakfast as it contains potatoes and can also work as a main meal with a salad.
You could add extra ingredients at step 4 – try a handful of peas, corn, diced red pepper, low-fat shredded cheese, or any combination.

Ingredients for
Spanish Omelet (serves 4)

• 1 lb. potatoes (peeled)
• 2 tablespoons olive oil
• 1 onion (finely chopped)
• 2 tablespoons water
• 4 eggs (beaten)

Serve slices of this
omelet hot or cold.

1. Cut the potatoes into ½ inch cubes.
2. Heat 1 tablespoon of oil in a large frying pan and fry the onions and potatoes for 5 minutes, stirring occasionally.
3. Add the water and cook on low heat for 15 minutes, or until the potatoes are soft.
4. Empty into a bowl and stir in the beaten eggs.
5. Heat the remaining tablespoon of oil in the frying pan and pour in the egg, onion and potato mixture.
6. Cook on low heat for 5–8 minutes.
7. To cook the top side, flip the omelet onto a plate and then back into the pan for 5 more minutes.

French toast

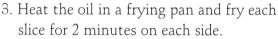

French toast, or 'eggy bread' is often popular with children. You could mix grated cheese into the egg for extra protein.

Ingredients for
French toast (serves 4)

• 2 eggs
• ½ cup milk
• 4 slices of bread
• a little olive oil

1. Beat the eggs and milk in a bowl.
2. Soak each slice of bread in the mixture.
3. Heat the oil in a frying pan and fry each slice for 2 minutes on each side.

You can cut the
slices of bread in
half before dipping,
or leave them whole.

Fruit and smoothies

Breakfast can be a good time to get more fruit into children's diets. When fresh berries are in season, try adding some to their cereal. During the colder months, dried fruit, such as apricots and raisins, can help sweeten oatmeal. Children who are reluctant to eat fruit may still be tempted by fruit smoothies and the vitamin content of the fruit is not affected by blending.

Fruit and nut boost

Fruit and yogurt go well together, but store-bought fruit yogurts often contain a lot of sugar. Instead, serve children a small bowl of plain yogurt and offer a range of fresh and dried fruit, nuts and seeds for them to sprinkle on themselves. To help boost fiber and carbohydrate intake, you could even try adding some bran and rolled oats. Drizzle a little honey or fruit compote (see page 106) over the mixture as a sweetener.

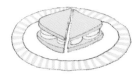

Banana sandwiches make a nutritious and filling start to the day.

Try adding any of these to a bowl of yogurt, cereal or oatmeal:

- sliced bananas
- sliced apples
- strawberries
- raspberries
- prunes
- dried apricots
- raisins
- chopped nuts
- granola

Here, yogurt has been topped with fresh peach slices, chopped pecans and a little honey.

Freezing fruit

Fruit, especially berries, can be expensive, but if you buy when a variety is in season, the prices are cheaper and the fruit usually tastes better too. It's worth buying a quantity of berries (from a pick-your-own farm, for example) when they're in season, and freezing some to use later in smoothies and compotes.

Breakfast drinks

It's important to rehydrate in the morning, so make sure children have a 6 oz. glass of water, milk or juice with their breakfast. Choose pure fruit juice, not fruit drinks that contain added sugar. Once opened, a carton of fruit juice begins to lose its vitamin C content after three days in the refrigerator.

Fruit smoothies

Smoothies can be made quickly from just milk, yogurt and bananas, but experiment with some other fruits and you'll soon come up with a few specials of your own. You can use fresh, frozen or canned fruits, but if opting for canned, choose fruits in natural juice rather than syrup.

1. Put everything in a blender and blend until smooth.

Encourage children to choose a piece of fruit to take to school.

Ingredients for Fruit smoothies
- *½ cup milk*
- *½ cup plain yogurt*
- *1 banana (sliced)*
- *handful of raspberries (fresh, frozen or canned)*
- *large slice of melon (skin removed, fruit cubed)*

Smoothies are high in vitamins, minerals and antioxidants.

Frozen berries don't have to be defrosted before you add them to the blender for a smoothie.

Crepes and pancakes

If you make the batter for crepes or pancakes the night before, they only take as long to cook as a piece of toast. They are also moderately low in fat, and you can control how much sugar goes onto them. All kinds of sweet toppings can be used. There are some ideas on the left.

Crepe and pancake toppings:

- apple, thinly sliced and fried in a tablespoon of butter
- maple syrup and pecans
- lemon juice and sugar
- mango and honey
- blueberries and whipped cream

Crepes

Ingredients for Crepes (serves 4)

- 1 cup all-purpose flour (sifted)
- 1 egg (beaten)
- 1 cup milk
- 1 teaspoon butter

1. Place the flour in a bowl and make a well in the middle.
2. Add the egg and pour in the milk gradually, mixing to form a smooth batter.
3. Leave to stand for at least half an hour before using.
4. Melt 1 teaspoon of butter in a frying pan and pour in a ladleful of batter. When the sides begin to set, shake the crepe and flip it over with a spatula.
5. Cook for 1 minute and serve.

You leave batter to stand so the starch in the flour can expand and the protein in the egg can 'relax'.

If you are feeling brave, try tossing your crepes instead of flipping them with a spatula.

Pancakes

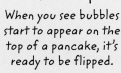

Useful tip

When you see bubbles start to appear on the top of a pancake, it's ready to be flipped.

To make pancakes, add two teaspoons of baking soda to the mix, which will make them puff up. Be aware that this is adding sodium, though (see page 28) so only make these occasionally. Make pancakes smaller than crepes, using only half a ladleful of batter for each one. You can usually cook three at a time in a medium-sized pan.

Lunch recipes

There are many healthy foods that can be
put together reasonably quickly for children's
lunches, whether they are going to eat the meal
at home, or take it to school or on an outing.
This section includes ideas for pasta, pizzas, salads,
soups, dips, sandwiches and wraps, along with
some easy fish dishes.

At a glance

Make your own dips to cut down on the oil content
and serve with raw vegetables or pita bread.

Try to vary the bread you use for sandwiches. If you have
time, or a bread machine, you could even make your own.

Homemade soups fill children up, and, if blended,
are a good way to disguise vegetables.

Fish is high in protein and generally takes very little time
to cook, so is ideal to include in lunchtime meals.

Try using leftover ingredients from the night
before to make quick pasta or rice salads.

Sandwiches and wraps

Sandwiches are easy to make and there is a wide range of breads that can be used, from plain sliced wheat to French baguettes, Italian ciabatta, German rye breads, tortilla wraps, bagels and pita bread. If you want to try making your own bread or rolls, there is a recipe on page 76.

Try to vary the bread you use as well as sandwich fillings.

• *Make sure you provide a bottle of water or half-and-half juice and water.*

• *Seal sandwiches in resealable zipper bags so they don't get wet from the ice pack or drinks.*

• *Supply a few pieces of carrot and cucumber with a container of hummus.*

• *Include one small treat a day such as a fun-sized chocolate bar or pudding snack.*

Lunch-box tips

Sandwiches are often the staple of packed lunches for school and picnics. To keep them fresh and cool, put an ice pack at the bottom of the box, or a small frozen carton of juice (it should be unfrozen and ready to drink by lunchtime). On the left are some more tips for making packed lunches.

It's a good idea not to use too many high-fat spreads on children's sandwiches, such as butter or regular mayonnaise. Instead use low-fat or fat-free mayonnaise, cheeses or homemade hummus (see page 69). Below are a few ideas for fillings to try:

• *turkey and low-fat swiss cheese*
• *hummus and roasted peppers*
• *grated cheese and carrot*
• *ham and lettuce*
• *tuna fish in water and light mayonnaise*

• *oven-roasted chicken breast*
• *chicken, avocado and low-fat plain yogurt*
• *peanut butter and banana*
• *avocado, grated cheese and carrot*

Chicken fajita wraps

Ingredients for
Chicken fajita wraps
(serves 4)

- juice of half a lime
- 2 tablespoons honey
- 1/2 teaspoon oregano
- pinch of ground cinnamon
- 1/2 teaspoon ground paprika
- 1 tablespoon canola oil
- 4 skinless, boneless chicken breasts
- 6 green onions (trimmed)
- 1 carrot (peeled)
- 1 red pepper (deseeded)
- 1 yellow pepper (deseeded)
- 8 soft flour tortillas

1. In a bowl, mix together the lime, honey, oregano, cinnamon and paprika, and a teaspoon of the oil.
2. Cut each chicken breast into eight strips, and then add the chicken to the bowl and mix well.
3. Cut the green onions, carrot, red pepper and yellow pepper into long, thin strips.
4. Heat the oven to 400°F.
5. Heat the oil in a frying pan and fry the chicken for 5 minutes, or until cooked, then remove from the pan.
6. Add the carrots to the pan and cook for 2 minutes. Add the green onions and peppers and cook for 2 minutes.
7. Return the chicken to the pan and put the tortillas in the oven for 2 minutes, to warm.
8. Put some of the chicken and vegetables in the middle of each tortilla, leaving the bottom half and sides empty. Fold the bottom half over the filling and wrap the sides tightly around it.

Children may enjoy assembling these fajita wraps.

Chicken fajitas are good for parties and picnics, too. Try adding extra ingredients, such as hummus or salsa.

Potato wedges (see page 93) are good for dipping.

Dips

Dips are easily available in supermarkets, but may contain preservatives and a lot of oil, whereas if you make your own, you can control how much goes into them. Dips can be eaten with cut-up vegetables and any kind of bread, but slices of pita work particularly well. (To make your own pitas, see the recipe on page 77.)

Tzatziki

Ingredients for Tzatziki

- 1 whole cucumber
- 1 1/2 cups plain low-fat yogurt
- 1 tablespoon fresh mint (chopped)
- juice of half a lemon

Tzatziki is a Greek and Turkish appetizer often served with warmed pita bread. Grated zucchini can also be used in place of the cucumber.

1. Peel the cucumber, cut in half, then cut again lengthways and scoop out the seeds with a spoon.
2. Grate or dice the cucumber, wrap in a clean dish towel and squeeze out any excess water.
3. Return to the bowl and mix with the yogurt, then stir in the mint and lemon juice.

Strips of pita bread, pepper, carrot or even lettuce work well for scooping up Tzatziki.

Hummus

Hummus contains tahini (sesame seed paste), which contains high levels of calcium. It can be bought from health-food stores and some supermarkets. Use the light rather than the dark variety, as it has a milder taste.

Ingredients for Hummus

- *14 oz. can chickpeas (in unsalted water)*
- *2 tablespoons water*
- *1 tablespoon tahini*
- *clove of garlic (crushed)*
- *juice of 1 lemon*
- *1 tablespoon olive oil*

1. Drain and rinse the chickpeas, then blend in a blender or food processor with the water until smooth.
2. Add the tahini, garlic, lemon juice and olive oil, and mix well. (You may need to add a little more water to get the right consistency.)

Hummus can also be served with falafel (see page 99)...

...and in various sandwich fillings (see page 66).

Offer hungry children a bowl of hummus with carrot and celery sticks.

Guacamole

Guacamole is a Mexican dip, usually served with tortilla chips. For a spicier version, you can add a sprinkle of chili powder or a chopped fresh chili pepper and a couple of chopped, ripe tomatoes instead of the sour cream.

Ingredients for Guacamole

- *2 ripe avocados*
- *juice of 1 lime*
- *clove of garlic (crushed)*
- *2 tablespoons plain yogurt or low-fat sour cream*

1. Remove the peel and pit from the avocados and then roughly chop the flesh.
2. Put in a bowl with the lime and garlic, and mash with a fork until smooth.
3. Stir in the yogurt or sour cream and serve.

Baked potatoes

Baked potatoes make a simple and satisfying meal – as long as you remember to put them in the oven in plenty of time. The fillings are quick and easy to prepare and generally nutritious.

If you can, use organic potatoes and scrub them thoroughly before you cook them, as potato skins are edible and contain useful vitamins and minerals. Prick the potatoes with a fork or push metal skewers through them to stop the skins from bursting in the oven.

For young children, scoop out the inside of a hot potato and mash it with a fork before returning it to the skin.

Older children may enjoy adding their own fillings so provide a selection for them to choose from.

Dry the potatoes with a paper towel before you prick the skins.

Ideas for toppings

- grated cheese
- cottage cheese
- low-fat sour cream
- canned tuna and a little reduced-fat mayonnaise mixed together
- baked beans (use low-salt and sugar variety, warmed in a pan)
- pesto (page 81) sprinkled with Parmesan cheese
- coleslaw

Cooking times

A potato the size of an adult fist will take about 45 minutes to an hour in the top of a hot oven at 425°F. To save time, you could microwave your potatoes for three minutes before putting them in the oven. Or microwave for about 4-7 minutes to fully cook a potato, then let it sit for a few minutes once it's done to allow it to finish cooking. Next cut the potatoes in half and, using oven gloves, squeeze the two sides to loosen up the insides. Add a spoonful of any of the toppings on the left.

Coleslaw

Coleslaw goes well with baked potatoes and, if children like it, it's an easy way to get them eating raw vegetables. All you have to do is put all of the ingredients listed on the left in a bowl and mix well.

As well as the basic ingredients, try adding any of the following to coleslaw...

• raisins
• green onions (chopped)
• red onion (finely chopped)
• chives (chopped)
• apple (peeled and grated)
• pinch of black pepper

Children could help with grating and mixing.

The tuna debate

Canned tuna is often suggested as a filling for baked potatoes or sandwiches, but there's some controversy surrounding the mercury levels found in the fish, as well as the fishing methods used. During the last decade there has been a devastating decline in tuna stocks due to industrial fishing methods, which have also caused the deaths of thousands of dolphins trapped inside the tuna nets.

Canned tuna is, however, a good source of low-fat protein and contains useful levels of B vitamins as well as phosphorus and selenium. So, if tuna is popular with your child, you could serve it occasionally as part of a healthy diet. Look for the dolphin-friendly logo on cans, and, wherever possible, buy 'line-caught' canned tuna.

Useful tip
Make tuna mayonnaise a healthier option by replacing the mayonnaise with natural yogurt and a squeeze of lemon juice.

Soups

Soups are another good way to get vegetables into children's diets and some kinds, such as leeks, carrots, broccoli and potatoes, can be turned into soup within half an hour. All of these recipes are suitable for vegetarians.

1. To make vegetable broth, chop two carrots, two leeks and two celery sticks.

All kinds of different vegetables can go into soups.

2. Put them in a pan of water with a teaspoon of black peppercorns, two bay leaves, and a handful of parsley.

3. Bring to a boil and simmer for an hour, then strain and use as needed.

Some of these soup recipes include a teaspoon of vegetable broth granules. Store-bought broth is usually high in salt, so don't be tempted to add more. Many stores now sell low-salt bouillon cubes or broth which are healthier options. To avoid salt entirely, try the recipe on the left to make broth that you can freeze and also use when you need it.

Potato soup

Ingredients for
Potato soup
(serves 4)

- 2 lbs. leeks
- 8 oz. potatoes
- 1 teaspoon vegetable broth granules, or 1 bouillon cube
- 2 cups cold water
- $\frac{1}{2}$ teaspoon nutmeg (freshly grated)
- dollop of plain yogurt
- chopped parsley or chives

1. Peel and roughly chop the leeks and potatoes and put them into a saucepan.
2. Add the vegetable bouillon and cold water.
3. Bring to a boil and simmer for around 30 minutes.
4. Take off the heat and leave to cool, then blend in a blender or food processor until smooth.
5. Pour back into the saucepan and add more water, if it is too thick, and the grated nutmeg.
6. Warm through and serve. For extra flavor, add a dollop of plain yogurt and a sprinkling of chives or parsley.

Roasted squash soup

Ingredients for
Roasted squash soup
(serves 4)

- 1 butternut squash
- 1 onion
- 2 tablespoons olive oil
- 3 cups cold water
- 1 teaspoon vegetable
  bouillon cube or granules

You could serve the soup with a teaspoon of low-fat sour cream.

1. Preheat the oven to 375°F, then cut the squash into quarters with a sharp knife.
2. Remove the seeds and pulp with a spoon and use a vegetable peeler to remove the skin.
3. Cut the flesh into even-sized chunks, and then peel and chop the onion into large chunks.
4. Spread the squash and onion on a baking tray, drizzle with the olive oil and roast for 30 minutes, or until soft.
5. Stir in 2 tablespoons of water to collect up the cooking juices. Pour the contents into a saucepan, cover with the rest of the water and stir in the vegetable bouillon.
6. Bring to a boil and simmer for 10 minutes. Allow to cool a little before blending in a blender until smooth.

Lentil soup

Ingredients for
Lentil soup (serves 4)

- 9 oz. red lentils
- a little olive oil
- 1 onion (finely chopped)
- clove of garlic (finely chopped)
- small piece of fresh ginger (peeled and grated)
- 1 teaspoon ground cumin
- 1 teaspoon ground cilantro
- 1 teaspoon turmeric
- 3 cups cold water
- juice of half a lemon

1. Rinse the lentils in cold water several times.
2. Heat the oil in a saucepan and fry the onion, garlic and ginger until soft. Add the cumin, cilantro and turmeric.
3. Stir in the lentils and cover with the water.
4. Bring to a boil, then reduce heat and simmer for about 30 minutes until the lentils are soft, adding more water if needed. Stir in the lemon juice and serve.

To add more carbohydrates, serve soup with slices of whole-wheat bread.

Fish

Fish is quick to cook and high in protein, and oily fish, such as mackerel, salmon, sardines and anchovies, are also an important source of Omega-3 fatty acids (see page 19). Children can be reluctant to eat fresh fish if they are not used to it, but you may have more success if you involve them in choosing which fish to buy and in the cooking.

Mackerel, for example, can be grilled, poached, barbecued or oven-baked. For a quick lunch, buy fillets and grill them on a hot grill or in the broiler, skin-side up, for 3–4 minutes, or until the skin is crisp. Serve with lemon wedges and salad (couscous salad works well – see page 84) or some boiled new potatoes.

Mackerel can also be grilled whole, and will need 5 minutes on each side.

A crispy salad goes well with grilled fish.

> **Useful tip**
> When grilling fish, brush the skin with a little oil and cover the grill pan with a sheet of foil to prevent the fish from sticking.

Kedgeree

Try to use undyed (white) smoked haddock in this dish and add a handful of cooked peas, if you want, at step 3.

1. Poach the fish in the milk with the bay leaf for 6 minutes. Add more milk to cover the fish, if necessary.
2. Remove the fish and break into flakes using a fork. Discard any bones and skin.
3. Boil the rice, according to the package instructions, until soft then stir in the fish. (You can add a little of the milk to make it less dry if you want.)
4. Add the hard-boiled egg quarters.

> **Ingredients for Kedgeree**
>
> - 1 lb. smoked haddock
> - $1/2$ cup milk
> - 1 bay leaf
> - 8 oz. basmati rice
> - 2 hard-boiled eggs (cut into quarters)

Bruschetta with anchovies

Ingredients for Bruschetta with anchovies (serves 4)

- 4 thick slices of bread
- 2 cloves of garlic (peeled and halved)
- 4 oz. tomatoes (sliced)
- 4 oz. pickled anchovies
- sprig of parsley (chopped)

Bruschetta (pronounced 'brusketta') is best made with Italian ciabatta, or a bread of similar texture. If possible, use pickled anchovies (available at delicatessens) for this recipe rather than canned, and very ripe tomatoes.

1. Toast the bread and rub the garlic over one side.
2. Grill the tomato slices, then lay them on the toast.
3. Spread the anchovies over the tomatoes with a knife.
4. Grill for 1 minute and serve sprinkled with parsley.

Smoked salmon paté

Ingredients for Smoked salmon paté (serves 4)

- 12 oz. smoked salmon (chopped)
- 5 oz. low-fat cream cheese
- 1 lemon

You can use smoked mackerel fillets in place of salmon for this recipe, although they will need to be skinned, carefully deboned and flaked. For a slightly tastier version, add some grated lemon zest and black pepper. To make a smoother paté, which some children prefer, blend all the ingredients together in a food processor.

1. Put the chopped smoked salmon in a bowl.
2. Squeeze over the juice of half the lemon and add the cream cheese, mixing well with a fork.
3. Serve on toast or in sandwiches (for lunch boxes).

You could serve smoked salmon paté with a sprinkling of parsley, a lemon wedge and some salad.

It's important to use bread flour, or strong flour as it is also called, for dough.

Making bread

If you have time, making bread is fairly easy (especially if you have a bread machine) and something most children enjoy doing, too. Although the whole process sounds time-consuming, you can do other things while the dough is rising or cooking. The basic dough can be used to make a loaf or for rolls, pita bread and pizza crusts.

Children may enjoy making and kneading dough.

Basic bread dough

Ingredients for Basic bread dough
- 4 cups bread flour (sifted)
- 1 teaspoon salt
- 1 teaspoon sugar
- a package (1 teaspoon) rapid-rise yeast
- 1 cup tepid water
- 1 tablespoon olive oil

For step 4, cover the bowl with a dish towel or clingfilm.

1. Put the flour, salt, sugar and yeast into a bowl and make a well in the middle. Pour in the warm water and oil. (Don't use hot water, as this will kill the yeast.)
2. Mix the ingredients into a dough. You may need to add more water to get the right consistency, but only do this a drop at a time as it's easy to add too much.
3. Roll up your sleeves, scatter flour over a clean worktop and put the dough on it. Use the heels of your hands to push the dough away from you firmly, then fold it in half and turn it around. Continue kneading in this way for 10 minutes, until it feels smooth and springy.
4. Put the dough in a large bowl, cover the bowl and leave the dough to rise in a warm, draft-free area for about 1 hour or until doubled in size.
5. Knead again for a few minutes.

Bread loaf

1. After the second knead (step 5 of basic bread dough), place the dough in an oiled 1 lb. loaf pan and leave to rise for the second time.
2. Heat the oven to 400°F.
3. Bake loaf for 25–30 minutes. (To see if ready, tap the bottom of the loaf. If it makes a hollow sound, it's done.)
4. Remove from the pan and allow to cool on a rack.

There are some ideas for sandwich fillings on page 66.

Bread rolls

You could add chopped olives to the dough or sprinkle seeds, instead of flour, over these rolls before cooking.

1. After you've kneaded the dough the second time (step 5 of basic bread dough), divide it into eight equal pieces.
2. Form the pieces into rolls. Place them on a lightly oiled baking tray and leave to rise for 20 minutes.
3. Heat the oven to 400°F.
4. Brush rolls with milk and dust with all-purpose flour. Bake for 10–15 minutes, or until golden on top.

Useful tip

To make herb rolls, add dried or chopped fresh herbs such as rosemary and sage to the dry ingredients before mixing the dough.

These rolls had sesame, poppy or sunflower seeds sprinkled on them.

Pita bread

1. Preheat the oven to 400°F.
2. Once the dough has risen (step 4 of basic dough), divide it into ten pieces and roll them into flat oval shapes.
3. Place the ovals on warm, lightly oiled baking trays and cook in the oven for 10 minutes.

Cut pizzas into slices with a pizza cutter or sharp knife.

Pizzas

Pizzas are fun for children to make and can provide a well-balanced meal. Store-bought or takeout pizzas are usually high in fat. This mainly comes from the cheese but also from oil in the dough. With homemade pizzas you can control the amount of cheese and oil you add and offer healthy toppings for children to choose from.

Pizza crust

1. Make the basic bread dough and once the dough has risen (step 4), divide it into four equal pieces.
2. Roll out each one into a circle 8 inches in diameter.
3. Place on a warmed, oiled baking tray, ready for topping.

Ingredients for
Pizza crust

• 1 quantity basic bread dough (see page 76)

Time-saving tips

• You could make your pizza crusts and tomato sauce in advance and store them in the refrigerator.

• You can buy ready-made pizza sauce in bottles or jars.

Tell children to roll out the dough to the thickness of their fingers.

Tomato sauce

Ingredients for
Tomato sauce

• 1 tablespoon olive oil
• 1 onion (finely chopped)
• clove of garlic (crushed)
• 14 oz. can chopped tomatoes
• 1 tablespoon fresh basil leaves (torn)

1. Heat the oil in a frying pan and fry the onion and garlic until soft. Add the tomatoes and stir well.
2. Just before the sauce boils, turn down the heat and simmer for at least 30 minutes, stirring occasionally. (The longer you cook this sauce, the better it tastes.) The result should be a thick tomato sauce.
3. Leave the mixture to cool, then stir in the basil leaves.

Building the pizza

1. Preheat the oven to 425°F.
2. On an 8 inch pizza crust, smooth over the tomato sauce with the back of a spoon to about ½ inch clear of the edge of the crust.
3. Lay on your toppings, spreading them out evenly and sprinkle on the grated cheese.
4. Cook pizzas for about 12 minutes, until the edges begin to turn golden and the cheese starts to melt.

Put out a selection of toppings and let children choose their own.

Ingredients for One 8 inch Pizza

- 1 pizza crust (see opposite)
- 1 tablespoon tomato sauce (see opposite)
- your choice of toppings (see below)
- 2 tablespoons grated cheese (a mixture of mozzarella and cheddar works well)

Topping ideas

- mushroom and pepper
- tomato and pesto
- olive and anchovy
- ham and pineapple
- chicken and red onion
- shrimp and cherry tomato
- olive and pine nut
- eggplant and arugula
- spinach and egg
- asparagus

Seafood toppings are a good source of protein.

Shrimp, Calamari (squid), Mussels, Cockles, Anchovy fillets, Canned sardines

Keeping it simple

It may be that a plain tomato base and a sprinkling of cheese are all children want, but this is fine. They will be getting carbohydrates from the bread, important vitamins from the tomato sauce and essential fats and protein from the cheese. As long as they eat a piece of fruit or some salad as well, they'll be eating a balanced meal.

Quick pizza toasties

Instead of a pizza crust, you could use whole-wheat (English) muffins, bread rolls or a baguette cut in half and toasted lightly on both sides. Place some slices of ripe tomato on top and add whatever you want – a few slices of mushroom perhaps, or some sliced olives. Sprinkle lightly with cheese and grill until bubbling.

Pasta lunches

Using different pasta shapes is an easy way to add variety to meals.

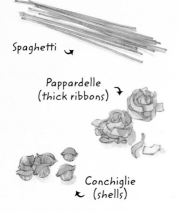

Spaghetti ↘

Pappardelle (thick ribbons) ↗

Conchiglie ↙ (shells)

Elicoidali ↙

Garganelli (squares rolled into a tube) ↙

Fusilli ↙

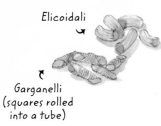

Macaroni ↙

Fusilli and macaroni both work well for the mix and match pasta dish.

Pasta is quick to cook and often so popular with children that it would be easy to serve it every day. If you keep a range of dried pasta shapes, children can choose which they want. Many of the best Italian pasta sauces are very simple and you don't need to cook anything apart from the pasta itself.

The secret of good pasta is making sure you use a large pan and plenty of boiling water. Some people add a few drops of oil to the water to help stop the pasta from sticking. After you've added the pasta to the water, stir it once and make sure you don't overcook it – follow the timing on the package. Drain well before adding sauce.

Mix and match pasta

You could serve a bowl of cooked pasta, tossed in a little olive oil, together with a selection of different ingredients, so children can mix their own lunch. Here are some to try:

- chopped ham
- toasted pine nuts
- grated cheese
- sun-dried tomatoes
- canned tuna

- cherry tomato halves
- chopped olives
- kidney beans
- corn
- feta cheese

Useful tip

To see if pasta is cooked, lift out a piece on a spoon, rinse it under cold water and bite it. It should be tender ('al dente') but not soggy.

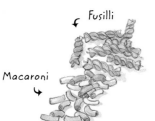

Pesto

Pesto sauce is a very useful standby. You can buy it in jars, but it's easy to make (if you can get fresh basil), and will last in the refrigerator for a few weeks in a sealed container. You only need about a heaped teaspoon of pesto per serving for children, as it has a strong, rich flavor. It works well with penne or fusilli.

Ingredients for
Pesto

- *2 oz. fresh basil leaves*
- *half a clove of garlic*
- *1 oz. pine nuts*
- *4 tablespoons olive oil*
- *2 tablespoons Parmesan cheese (grated)*
- *2 teaspoons lemon juice*

1. Put the basil, garlic, pine nuts and half the oil into a blender and blend into a smooth paste.
2. Pour the paste into a jar and stir in the rest of the oil, Parmesan and lemon juice.

You could use a pestle and mortar to pound together the pesto ingredients.

You can grow basil and other herbs in pots on a sunny windowsill.

Anchovy and carrot sauce

This may sound like a strange combination, but don't be put off, as this is a very tasty sauce and another way to get oily fish into a meal. You will find the canned anchovies 'melt' into the sauce as they cook. Spaghetti works particularly well for the pasta.

Ingredients for
Anchovy and carrot sauce

- *1 tablespoon olive oil*
- *1 onion (finely chopped)*
- *clove of garlic (finely chopped)*
- *1 lb. carrots (peeled and grated)*
- *14 oz. can chopped tomatoes*
- *2 oz. can anchovy fillets (drained)*

1. Heat the oil in a frying pan and fry the onion for about 5 minutes.
2. Add the garlic and continue to cook for 1 minute.
3. Stir in the grated carrots, then the tomatoes and anchovy fillets, and cook for about 40 minutes.
4. Serve with your pasta of choice.

Pasta and rice salads

Pasta and rice salads make good use of leftover ingredients but are also worth making from scratch for packed lunches and picnics. On these pages are some recipe ideas that you can adapt easily for variety. The trick is not to put too many different ingredients together, as this can spoil the overall taste.

Some pasta or rice salad combinations to try:

- *hard-boiled egg and fish (tuna or salmon work well)*

- *Waldorf salad: apples, raisins, celery and walnuts*

- *'traffic lights': cherry tomatoes, corn and peas*

Pasta and rice salads travel well so are good to take on a picnic.

Safety point

Rice can contain the bacteria Bacillus cereus which causes vomiting and diarrhea. Always store cooked rice in the refrigerator promptly, and use within three days.

Preparing rice or pasta

Cook the rice or pasta, drain, then rinse with cold water. (This is important otherwise it will keep cooking and become soggy.) Stir in a tablespoon of olive oil and a good squeeze of lemon, mixing thoroughly. This will help to prevent the grains or pieces from sticking together. Now you can stir in any of the fillings on these two pages.

Chicken and corn salad

Ingredients for Chicken and corn salad

- *juice of 1 lemon*
- *1 skinless, boneless chicken breast*
- *1/2 cup corn (canned or frozen)*
- *sprinkling of paprika*

This recipe works well with either pasta or rice.

1. Preheat the oven to 375°F.
2. Place the chicken on a piece of foil and squeeze over the lemon juice. Wrap it up and cook for about 30 minutes.
3. When cool, cut into small cubes and mix with the rice or pasta, corn and a sprinkling of paprika.

Carrot and sunflower seed salad

This recipe works best with pasta. Toasted pine nuts can be used instead of the toasted sunflower seeds.

1. Preheat the oven to 350°F.
2. Place the sunflower seeds on a baking tray and toast in the oven for about 10 minutes, stirring occasionally. (Alternatively you can dry-fry them in a pan on the stove until browned.)
3. Sprinkle the grated carrot onto the pasta and stir in the sunflower seeds.
4. Squeeze in the orange juice and finish with a sprinkling of chopped parsley.

*Ingredients for
Carrot and sunflower
seed pasta salad*

- *¼ cup sunflower seeds*
- *1 carrot (peeled and grated)*
- *juice of 1 orange*
- *sprig of parsley (chopped)*

You could add a little grated ginger to the orange juice.

Rice and bean salad

Any canned beans can be used here, but cannellini and navy beans are mild in flavor and soak up the flavor of the dressing well. This recipe works best with rice.

1. Drain the cannellini beans and rinse in cold water.
2. Stir into the rice together with the orange juice, cherry tomato quarters, cucumber and parsley.

*Ingredients for
Rice and bean salad*

- *14 oz. can cannellini (or other) beans*
- *juice of 1 orange*
- *11 oz. cherry tomatoes (quartered)*
- *1 medium cucumber (diced)*
- *1 teaspoon fresh parsley*

Cucumber and beans provide texture and crunch in this rice and bean salad.

Couscous swells up and becomes light and fluffy as it absorbs liquid.

Couscous

Couscous is a staple ingredient of North African cooking. It is made from grains of semolina and is often eaten with grilled or stewed meat, fish, or vegetables, although it makes a delicious salad too. Couscous is high in carbohydrates, low in fat, and a good source of selenium, which boosts the immune system.

Couscous salad

Ingredients for Couscous salad (serves 4)

- 1 teaspoon bouillon granules
- 1 cup boiling water
- 3 tablespoons canola oil
- 8 green onions (chopped)
- 8 oz. couscous
- 2 tablespoons lemon juice
- 4 ripe tomatoes (deseeded and chopped)
- half a cucumber (deseeded and diced)
- 1 yellow pepper (deseeded and chopped)
- 4 tablespoons fresh mint (chopped)

1. Dissolve the bouillon in the boiling water.
2. Put 1 tablespoon of the oil and the green onions in a saucepan and fry for 1 minute, then pour in the broth and heat until boiling.
3. Remove the pan from the heat and stir in the couscous. Cover and leave for 3 minutes, or until all of the liquid is absorbed.
4. For the dressing, in a bowl mix together the 2 remaining tablespoons of oil, the lemon juice and a little black pepper.
5. Spoon the couscous into a large bowl and pour over the dressing. Mix well with a fork and leave to cool.
6. Stir in the tomatoes, cucumber, pepper and mint.

You could serve the couscous on some mixed salad leaves.

Main meals

Many children eat their main meal in the evening, but some people are often hesitant to cook much for dinner, due to busy schedules and restless, hungry children. Most of the healthy meals here, however, only take about 30 to 40 minutes to prepare and cook, especially if you can get into the habit of making certain things in advance.

At a glance

Tomato sauce can form the basis of many meals, so it's a good idea to make it in large batches and freeze some.

Homemade chicken or fish fingers and potato wedges are surprisingly easy to make, and much healthier than the store-bought or restaurant varieties.

Stir-fries are a quick and healthy standby.

Oven temperatures can vary from oven to oven, so the times and temperatures given here may need adjusting slightly to suit your oven.

A few simple ingredients go into making tomato sauce and you can use dried herbs if you don't have fresh ones.

Spinach, zucchini, carrots and green onions can all be 'hidden' in tomato sauce.

Tomato-based recipes

A good tomato sauce is the basis for many meals. It can be used on pasta and pizzas and as part of a meat sauce, as well as in the recipes given here. For each of these dishes, you'll need to make a quantity of the tomato sauce on page 78. If you have a deep freeze, it's worth making the sauce in bulk and freezing it in 8 oz. containers. Take the sauce out of the freezer the night before and you will have the makings of a main meal when you need it.

For the tomato sauce recipe and to find out how to use it on pizzas, see page 78.

It's easy to add other vegetables to tomato sauce, especially when using it as a base for something else. Try adding a red pepper, seeded and diced, to the sauce. Celery, spinach, onions and leeks can be used too. They will all disappear completely if you liquidize the sauce.

Eggplant bake

Ingredients for Eggplant bake (serves 4)

- 2 eggplants (cut into $1/2$ inch slices)
- 1 quantity of tomato sauce (see above)
- 3 tablespoons fresh basil leaves (torn)
- good handful of cheese (cheddar, mozzerella or Parmesan work well)

1. Preheat the oven to 350°F.
2. Simmer the eggplant slices in a pan of boiling water for 4 minutes. Remove and pat dry with a paper towel.
3. Spoon a little of the tomato sauce into the bottom of an oven-proof dish and layer the eggplants on top.
4. Season with a good pinch of black pepper.
5. Stir the torn basil leaves into the remaining tomato sauce and pour over the layered eggplant.
6. Scatter the cheese on top and bake in the oven for 35–40 minutes. Serve with crusty bread and a side salad.

Quick chickpea casserole

*Ingredients for
Chickpea casserole (serves 4)*

- *2 quantities of tomato sauce (page 78)*
- *14 oz. can chickpeas*
- *½ cup corn*

1. Pour the tomato sauce into a saucepan.
2. Drain and rinse the chickpeas and add to the pan.
3. Stir in the corn (you could add a handful of chopped spinach here too) and warm through.
4. Serve with brown rice or couscous.

Chicken casserole

*Ingredients for
Chicken casserole (serves 4)*

- *1 tablespoon olive oil*
- *4 boneless and skinless chicken breasts*
- *1 quantity of tomato sauce (page 78)*
- *2 carrots (peeled and sliced)*
- *1 cup peas (fresh or frozen)*

This dish can also be made with beef, pork or lamb. If using any of these alternatives, dice the meat into 1 inch cubes and allow 10 minutes extra oven-cooking time.

1. Preheat the oven to 400°F.
2. Heat the oil in a frying pan and add the chicken. Fry for 5 minutes, turning a few times, until no pink juice comes out.
3. Warm the tomato sauce in a casserole dish with a lid and add the chicken and carrots.
4. Put into the oven and cook for 25 minutes.
5. Remove from the oven and stir in the peas.
6. Return to the oven and cook for 5 more minutes.

Serve the casserole with mashed potatoes and whole-grain bread.

Meat sauce

Meat sauce is extremely versatile. It can be served with pasta or become part of a lasagne or shepherd's pie. Use sliced mushrooms and finely diced carrots or a combination of chopped vegetables in place of the ground beef to make vegetarian versions of these recipes.

1. Heat the oil in a pan, add the onion and fry until soft.
2. Add the ground beef and fry until brown.
3. Carefully drain any grease from the meat.
4. Pour in the tomato sauce, mix well and simmer for 30–40 minutes, stirring from time to time.
5. Serve with pasta and a sprinkling of fresh parsley.

Ingredients for Meat sauce (serves 4)

- 1 tablespoon olive oil
- 1 onion (finely chopped)
- 1 lb. lean ground beef
- 1 quantity of tomato sauce (see page 78)
- 1 tablespoon fresh parsley (chopped)

To make a meat sauce go further, add ¾ cup (3 ½ oz.) of rinsed red lentils at step 3.

Show children how to twirl spaghetti around a fork.

Cheese sauce

This cheese sauce forms a layer in the lasagne recipe opposite, but it can also be poured over cauliflower, broccoli or cooked macaroni and lightly baked.

1. Heat the oil in a saucepan and add the flour. Stir continuously over the heat for 2 minutes.
2. Pour in the milk gradually, stirring continuously to prevent lumps from forming.
3. Continue to stir over the heat until the sauce thickens.
4. Remove from the heat and stir in the grated cheese.

Ingredients for Cheese sauce

- 2 tablespoons olive oil
- 1 tablespoon all-purpose flour
- 1 cup milk
- ½ cup (2 oz.) cheddar cheese (grated)

Lasagne

Ingredients for
Lasagne (serves 4)

• 2 quantities of meat
 sauce (see left)
• 6 oz. dried lasagne sheets
• 1 quantity of cheese sauce
 (see below left)

To make an extra deep
lasagne, you could add a
third layer of everything.

1. Preheat the oven to 400°F.
2. Spoon half of the meat sauce over the bottom of a shallow, rectangular oven-proof dish and spread it out into an even layer.
3. Boil the lasagne sheets as directed on the package, then cover the layer of meat sauce with a single layer of lasagne sheets, cutting them up if necessary to cover the area fully.
4. Pour half of the cheese sauce over the lasagne sheets, smoothing it into an even layer with the back of a spoon.
5. Add the remainder of the meat sauce and then another layer of lasagne sheets.
6. Pour on the rest of the cheese sauce, smooth it out and bake the lasagne in the oven for 25 minutes.

Shepherd's pie

Ingredients for
Shepherd's pie
(serves 4)

• 3 ½ oz. red lentils
• 2 quantities of meat
 sauce (see above left)
• 2 lbs. potatoes (peeled)
• 4 tablespoons milk

1. Preheat the oven to 400°F.
2. Rinse the lentils in a sieve under cold running water.
3. Warm the meat sauce and stir in the lentils.
4. Keep on the heat until the lentils have softened and burst. (This should take about 15 minutes.)
5. Meanwhile, cut the potatoes into roughly 2 inch cubes and put into a saucepan of water. Boil until very soft, then drain and return to the pan.
6. Pour in the milk and mash until smooth.
7. Spoon the meat sauce into an oven-proof dish and spread out evenly.
8. Add small spoonfuls of mashed potatoes on top at even intervals.
9. Smooth over evenly with a spatula and then drag a fork across the top to make little ridges.
10. Place in the oven and cook for about 25 minutes, or until golden brown.

Both the meat sauce and
mashed potatoes can be made
ahead of time for this recipe.

Roasted chicken and vegetables

This is a fairly easy dish to make and if you drain the fat off the pan before you make gravy, and remove the skin before you serve the chicken, also a healthy one.

Roasted chicken

1. Preheat the oven to 400°F.
2. Remove any string tying the chicken's legs together.
3. Push the lemon halves, thyme and bay leaf inside the chicken cavity and rub the oil all over the chicken.
4. Put the chicken in a roasting pan, wash your hands well, and cook in the oven for 45 minutes.
5. Remove from the oven and carefully tip the cavity so the juices run out. Spoon them over the chicken to baste it.
6. Return to the oven and cook for 45 more minutes.
7. Allow the chicken to 'rest' on a plate, covered in foil, for 10 minutes before carving.

Ingredients for Roasted chicken

- 1 roasting chicken, about 3 1/2 lbs.
- 1 lemon (halved)
- sprig of fresh thyme
- 1 bay leaf
- 1 tablespoon canola oil

To check if a chicken is cooked, pierce the thickest part of the leg with a skewer until the juices run out. They shouldn't have any pink or red in them.

Most children look forward to a roasted meal.

Making gravy

1. Carefully spoon off the fat from the roasting pan that contained the chicken. It will be clear and will have settled on top of the brown chicken juices.
2. Put the pan over low heat and stir in the flour, mustard and vegetable granules or cube.
3. Continue to stir, gradually adding the water, and heat until bubbling.

Ingredients for Gravy

- roasted chicken juices
- 1 tablespoon all-purpose flour
- 1 teaspoon dijon mustard
- 1 bouillon cube, or 1 teaspoon granules
- 1 cup boiling water

Roasted vegetables

Ingredients for
Roasted vegetables

• 1 lb. potatoes (peeled)
• ¹/₂ lb. carrots (peeled)
• ¹/₂ lb. onions (peeled)
• ¹/₂ lb. butternut
  squash (peeled)
• 2 tablespoons olive oil
• sprig fresh thyme
• sprig fresh rosemary

1. Preheat oven to 400°F.
2. Cut the potatoes into halves if they are small, or quarters if they are large. Cut the carrots, onions and squash into 2 inch pieces.
3. Heat the oil in a baking tray and add the vegetables, stirring until all have been touched by the oil.
4. Sprinkle over the thyme and rosemary leaves.
5. Place at the top of the oven for 1 hour, or until golden, turning at least once.

Useful tip

Cook the chicken for an extra 10 minutes if you are roasting vegetables at the same time, as the oven door will have been opened several times.

Steamed cauliflower goes well with chicken, but you might want to add a more colorful vegetable too.

For a lighter meal, serve rice or new potatoes and some lightly steamed vegetables with roasted chicken.

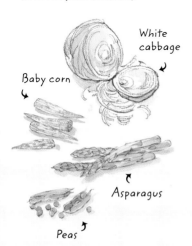

White cabbage

Baby corn

Asparagus

Peas

Uses for leftovers

If you have any chicken or vegetables left over after this meal, put them in a sealed container and refrigerate them for the next day. Here are a few ideas for things you could do with them:

• Cold chicken could be used in sandwiches or added to stir-fries.

• The carcass can be used to make broth (see page 72).

• You could use the roasted vegetables to make a salad.

Chicken fingers and potato wedges

Chicken tenders and French fries are often a favorite with children, but deep-fried, store-bought or restaurant versions, while fine for a treat, are much too fatty for regular eating. Follow the recipes here to cut down on the fat content.

Chicken fingers

Ingredients for
Chicken fingers (serves 4)

- 3 slices of whole-wheat bread
- handful parsley (chopped)
- 1 lb. boneless, skinless chicken breast
- juice of 1 lemon

1. Preheat oven to 400°F.
2. In a blender or food processor, blend the 3 slices of bread to make breadcrumbs, and then stir in the parsley.
3. Cut the chicken into strips roughly 1 x 4 inches.
4. Put the lemon juice into a bowl and dip in the chicken, then dunk it into the breadcrumbs making sure each strip is covered all over.
5. Place on a baking tray and cook in the oven for about 20 minutes, turning once halfway through.

You can use strips of white fish in place of the chicken for this recipe to make fish sticks.
Just decrease the cooking time by 5 minutes.

Useful tip

If you are serving the chicken with potato wedges (see opposite), wait until the wedges have been cooking for 25 minutes before putting the chicken in.

These fish sticks have been made with cod, but you could also use hake, haddock, coley or tuna.

Potato wedges

Ingredients for
Potato wedges (serves 4)

- 2 lbs. potatoes
- 4 tablespoons olive oil
- 2 tablespoons fresh
  rosemary (chopped)
- 2 tablespoons fresh
  sage (chopped)

If preparing wedges for dips
(see page 68), you could add
a sprinkling of spice, such as
paprika or ground cumin.

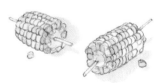

Fish sticks or chicken fingers
go well with corn on the cob
and homemade ketchup.

These take almost as long to cook as baked potatoes and a little longer to prepare, but they're healthier than French fries.

1. Preheat the oven to 400°F.
2. Wash the potatoes, leaving the skins on if they look good, removing them if they don't.
3. Cut the potatoes into quarters lengthways. If they are particularly large, cut each potato into six pieces. (You want the wedges to be chunky but not enormous.)
4. Put the wedges in a bowl, drizzle the oil over them and turn them until they are evenly coated. Stir in the herbs.
5. Put on a baking tray and cook at the bottom of the oven for about 45 minutes, turning them at least twice.

A well-balanced meal?

Chicken fingers and potato wedges are a good source of protein and carbohydrates, but you'll need to add some vegetables or salad to make this meal nutritionally balanced – perhaps some peas and carrots, a mixed salad, or some coleslaw (see page 71). There are some vegetables in the ketchup recipe below, too.

Homemade tomato ketchup

Ingredients for
Homemade ketchup

- 1 small red onion (finely
  chopped)
- clove of garlic (crushed)
- 14 oz. can chopped
  tomatoes

Most store-bought ketchup is very high in sugar, so, if you have time, it's a good idea to make your own. It will keep in the refrigerator for up to a week in a sealed container.

1. Put the red onion, garlic and tomatoes into a small saucepan and bring to a boil.
2. Simmer for 15–20 minutes, or until well reduced.
3. Leave to cool, then liquidize if you want a smooth sauce.

Fish dishes

All of these dishes can be prepared in advance, so they just need to go in the oven before serving.

Smoked salmon fishcakes

Ingredients for Fishcakes (serves 4)

- 1 lb. potatoes (peeled and chopped)
- 3 slices whole-wheat bread
- 12 oz. smoked salmon

1. Boil the potatoes until soft, then drain and mash.
2. Preheat the oven to 400°F.
3. Blend the bread in a blender to make breadcrumbs.
4. Cut the salmon into small squares and stir into the mash.
5. When cool enough to handle, divide the mixture into eight equal amounts and shape into fishcakes.
6. Coat in the breadcrumbs, place on a warmed baking tray and cook for 20 minutes, or until golden brown.

Serve fishcakes with some vegetables...

...or a salad, for a well-balanced meal.

Children could help by shaping the fishcakes.

Quick fish stew

Ingredients for Fish stew (serves 4)

- 1 tablespoon olive oil
- 1 onion (finely chopped)
- clove of garlic (finely chopped)
- 1 lb. white fish, ex. haddock (chunks)
- 2 quantities of tomato sauce (see page 78)
- 1 tablespoon fresh parsley (chopped)

1. Preheat the oven to 350°F.
2. Heat the oil in a frying pan over medium heat. Add the onion and fry until soft.
3. Add the garlic and cook for 2 more minutes.
4. Add the fish chunks to the pan and stir gently until lightly browned on both sides.
5. Spoon the fish mixture into an oven-proof dish.
6. Warm the tomato sauce through in a saucepan and pour it all over the fish. Heat in the oven for 15 minutes.
7. Sprinkle with parsley and serve with rice and salad.

Fish and shrimp casserole

Don't be discouraged by the long list of ingredients and steps for this dish; it's fairly quick and easy to prepare.

Ingredients for
Fish and shrimp casserole
(serves 4)

- 2 lbs. potatoes (peeled)
- 1 lb. haddock or other white fish (skinned and boned)
- 1 1/2 cups milk
- 1 teaspoon vegetable bouillon granules
- 1 bay leaf
- 6 green onions (thinly sliced)
- 1 tablespoon olive oil
- 1/2 cup all-purpose flour
- juice of half a lemon
- 2 tablespoons fresh parsley (chopped)
- 3 1/2 oz. peeled shrimp

You can buy shrimp precooked or raw. Raw are best for this recipe, as they can become rubbery if over-cooked.

1. Cut the potatoes into small chunks and boil them in a saucepan of water until soft, then drain and mash.
2. Preheat the oven to 400°F.
3. Put the haddock in a separate saucepan and cover with the milk. Add the broth granules and bay leaf.
4. Heat until just boiling, then reduce the heat and simmer for 5 minutes.
5. Remove the fish (retaining the milk for later) and allow to cool before breaking into flakes. Spread them out in a deep, medium-sized oven-proof dish.
6. Fry the green onions in the olive oil for a few minutes. Then add the flour, a little at a time, until it forms a thick paste.
7. Slowly pour in the milk from the fish, stirring until you have made a sauce. Then add the lemon juice and parsley and stir again.
8. Scatter the shrimp over the fish and pour the sauce on top, making sure everything is well covered.
9. Dot the mashed potatoes over the surface. Smooth evenly with a spatula and drag a fork across the top.
10. Cook in the oven for about 20 minutes, or until golden and bubbling.

Garnish the fish casserole with a sprig of parsley.

Rosti

Rosti is a dish in which potatoes are grated or thinly sliced and pan-fried. It is traditionally made with butter, but olive oil works just as well. Adding smoked haddock is another way to get more fish into children's diets.

Did you know?

Rosti is originally from Switzerland, where it roughly translates as 'crisp and golden'.

Older children can help with the grating, though a grating attachment on a food processor may be quicker.

Try to buy 'white' smoked haddock, rather than the dyed yellow variety, which contains food colorings.

Smoked haddock rosti

Ingredients for Smoked haddock rosti (serves 4)

- 1 lb. potatoes (grated)
- 1 onion (finely chopped)
- 2 cloves of garlic (finely chopped)
- 1 tablespoon olive oil
- 1 lb. smoked haddock (cut into thin slices)
- rind of half an unwaxed lemon (grated)
- 1 tablespoon fresh parsley (chopped)

1. Put the potatoes and onions into a colander and rinse well with cold water. Roll them up tightly in some paper towels to remove excess water.
2. Pour them into a bowl and add the chopped garlic.
3. Heat the oil in a frying pan on high heat and add half the potatoes, pressing down firmly.
4. Scatter the fish evenly on top and then sprinkle with the lemon rind and parsley. Top with the remaining potatoes and press down firmly again.
5. Cover with a lid and cook on the lowest heat for about 25–30 minutes.
6. Remove the lid, turn up the heat and cook for 5 more minutes. Brown the top of the rosti in the broiler for a few minutes and serve with salad.

Cheese rosti

Ingredients for
Cheese rosti (serves 4)

- 1 lb. potatoes (peeled and halved if large)
- 1 tablespoon olive oil
- 1 onion (finely chopped)
- ½ cup (2 oz.) cheese (grated)

1. Boil the potatoes for 10 minutes, or until just tender.
2. Drain, leave to cool and then grate the potatoes.
3. Heat the oil in a large frying pan, add the onions and cook for about 5 minutes, or until soft.
4. Add the potatoes, pressing the mixture down, and cook until well browned. Flip over and brown the other side.
5. Top with the grated cheese and place in the broiler, until the cheese has melted and turned golden.

Vegetable rosti

Ingredients for
Vegetable rosti (serves 4)

- 2 tablespoons olive oil
- 2 onions (finely chopped)
- 3 ½ oz. potatoes (peeled and grated)
- 3 ½ oz. sweet potatoes (peeled and grated)
- 3 ½ oz. zucchini (cut into fine strips)
- 2 tablespoons pine nuts (finely chopped)
- 1 egg (beaten)
- 2 tablespoons all-purpose flour

1. Heat the oil in a large frying pan, add the onion, potato, sweet potato, zucchini and pine nuts, and fry for about 5 minutes or until soft, stirring regularly.
2. Leave to cool a little, spoon into a bowl and stir in the egg yolk and flour.
3. Divide the mixture into 8 equal quantities and shape into balls, then flatten each one slightly.
4. Return the frying pan to the heat, adding a drop more oil if necessary, and cook the rosti in small batches until golden brown on each side.
5. Drain on paper towels and serve.

Homemade ketchup
(see page 93) and salad
goes well with rosti.

Sprinkle a little grated cheese on burgers, rather than adding a thick slice.

Burgers, kebabs and falafel

These high-protein foods can be eaten with a range of breads and salads. Burgers go well on bread rolls (see page 77) and kebabs and falafel can be eaten in pita bread. Serve them with shredded lettuce, diced tomatoes and cucumber and some hummus or tzatziki. You could serve the burgers with potato wedges instead of fries (see page 93).

Burgers

You can use ground turkey to make these burgers, too. Try experimenting with different herbs, such as sage with turkey or oregano with beef.

1. Put all the ingredients in a bowl and stir.
2. Divide the mixture into eight portions.
3. Roll each one into a ball, then press into burger shapes.
4. Cook on a grill or broiler for 10–12 minutes, turning them over regularly.
5. Serve on a whole-wheat bun or roll, with a little salad and homemade tomato ketchup (see page 93).

Ingredients for Burgers
(makes 8 small burgers)

• 1 lb. lean ground beef
• 1 onion (finely chopped)
• clove of garlic (crushed)
• 1 tablespoon fresh parsley (chopped)

You could serve these little burgers on homemade bread rolls (see page 77).

Shish kebabs

Ingredients for
Shish kebabs (makes 8)

- 1 ½ lbs. cube steak
- 2 tablespoons olive oil
- juice of 1 lemon
- clove of garlic (finely chopped)
- sprig of fresh rosemary (chopped)
- 8 metal or wooden skewers

1. Remove any fat and cut the meat into cubes about 1 inch across. Put them in a bowl and add the oil, lemon juice, garlic and rosemary.
2. Leave the meat to soak up these flavors for at least 1 hour (or overnight) in the refrigerator.
3. Put the meat onto the skewers.
4. Turn on the grill or broiler and cook the kebabs for 10–12 minutes, turning every so often.
5. Serve in pita bread with salad and tzatziki (see page 68).

You can also grill vegetables on the skewers with the meat for a complete meal.

If using wooden skewers for the kebabs, soak them in water for 20 minutes before use, as this will stop them from burning during cooking.

Falafel

Ingredients for
Falafel (serves 4)

- 14 oz. can chickpeas
- 2 tablespoons lemon juice
- 1 onion (very finely chopped)
- 2 cloves of garlic (crushed)
- 1 teaspoon ground cilantro
- 1 teaspoon ground cumin
- 1 tablespoon fresh parsley (finely chopped)
- 2 tablespoons all-purpose flour
- 1–2 tablespoons olive oil

1. Drain and rinse the chickpeas and lightly blend in a blender. The mixture should still be slightly coarse, like breadcrumbs, not a smooth purée.
2. Add the lemon juice, onion, garlic, cilantro, cumin and parsley and mix well.
3. Roll a small handful of the mixture into a ball, then flatten slightly. Repeat with the rest of the mixture.
4. Heat the oil in a frying pan and fry the falafel balls in batches for 2–3 minutes on each side.
5. Drain on paper towels. Serve in pita bread with a dollop of hummus (see page 69) and some salad.

Stir-fries

Stir-fries are quick and easy to make, and a whole range of ingredients can be used. They work best cooked in a wok, but, if you don't have one, a large frying pan will do.

Useful tip

For the stir-fries that have cooked rice in them, precooked and cooled basmati rice works best.

You can replace the meat with tofu (bean curd) marinated in soy sauce and grated ginger.

Chopped, unsalted cashew nuts are good for adding crunch to a stir-fry.

The secret of a good stir-fry is getting everything ready before you start cooking.

• Make sure your ingredients are all chopped and ready before you start.

• Cut meat and vegetables into thin strips, so they will cook evenly and quickly.

• Cook on high heat and make sure your pan is very hot before you begin.

Egg stir-fry

Ingredients for Egg stir-fry (serves 4)

• a little olive oil or butter
• 1 or 2 eggs (beaten)
• 1 lb. cooked rice
• your choice of extra ingredients

This is a good meal for older children to learn to cook and they can choose extra ingredients to add, such as strips of ham and carrots or some peas. If the idea of being able to cook their own meal grabs them, children may then want to experiment. You could even suggest they try adding some shredded spinach and grated zucchini.

1. Heat a little oil or butter in a frying pan. Pour in the egg and stir until scrambled.
2. Add the cooked rice and your extra ingredients, and stir until warmed through.

Shrimp stir-fry

You can also use chicken, turkey, pork or beef for this recipe. Cut the meat into thin strips and add to the pan with the vegetables at step 2, but make sure the meat is cooked thoroughly before serving.

Ingredients for
Shrimp stir-fry (serves 4)

- 1 red pepper (deseeded)
- ¹/₂ cup green beans
- 1 tablespoon olive oil
- 4 green onions (thinly sliced)
- ¹/₂ cup corn
- 9 oz. peeled shrimp (cooked)
- 1 lb. cooked rice

1. Cut the red pepper into thin strips. Snip the tips off the green beans and cut into small, equal-sized pieces.
2. Heat the oil in a frying pan and fry the red pepper, green beans, green onions and corn for about 5 minutes.
3. Add the shrimp and rice and warm through.
4. Serve with light soy sauce to taste.

The vegetable pak choy tastes good in stir-fries. Chop roughly and add toward the end.

Noodle stir-fries

Noodle stir-fries are even quicker and easier to make than rice ones, especially if you can get fresh noodles. Even dried noodles generally just need soaking for a few minutes in hot water before you add them. Cook the meat and vegetables as described above, but replace the rice with cooked noodles and finish with a splash of soy sauce.

Shrimp stir-fry
with noodles

Butternut squash, celery and asparagus are all delicious added to a risotto.

Ingredients for
Simple risotto (serves 4)

- 1 tablespoon olive oil
- 1 onion (finely chopped)
- 14 oz. Arborio rice
- 3 ¹/₂ cups hot vegetable broth
- ¹/₂ cup (2 oz.) Parmesan cheese (grated)
- 1 tablespoon fresh parsley (chopped)

You can add your choice of vegetables to a risotto 15 minutes into cooking. This one contains tomatoes, peas and broccoli.

Risotto

This way of cooking rice originated in Italy and the soft, creamy texture of a risotto often appeals to children. To make a risotto, you ladle hot broth into the rice, a little at a time, and stir continuously until cooked. You'll need to use Arborio rice, as this is what gives the risotto a creamy texture and nutty flavor.

Simple risotto

Risotto is often made with mushrooms, which you can add when the onions are soft (if your children like them). You could also try dried mushrooms, which need to be soaked in hot water for 10 minutes, then drained and roughly chopped. Add them at the end, before the parmesan cheese.

1. Heat the oil in a saucepan. Fry the onions until soft.
2. Add the rice and stir until it begins to go translucent.
3. Add a ladleful of broth and stir well until it is absorbed.
4. Continue adding ladlefuls of broth, stirring each time, until all the liquid is absorbed, which should take about 35 minutes.
5. When the rice is soft but still has a little texture, take the pan off the heat and stir in the cheese and parsley.

Drinks and desserts

Desserts and other sweet treats are fine once in a while, but it's still a good idea to make them yourself, so you can be sure they are as healthy as possible. All the recipes in this section have been chosen because they include fruit or other healthy ingredients. They also use on average 2 oz. (almost 5 tablespoons) less sugar than traditional recipes.

At a glance

Satisfy children's thirst for something more than just water or milk by making homemade milk shakes.

Increase children's fruit intake by including as much fruit as possible in desserts and drinks.

It's easy to make your own gelatin, and it's healthier than store-bought gelatin which has food coloring and lots of sugar in it.

Store-bought ice cream is often bulked up with vegetable oils and sugar. Make your own to control what goes into it.

Sponge cakes are high in fat, but also contain protein in the egg and carbohydrates in the flour, so are fine in moderation.

Try using whole-wheat flour in fruit scones and bran flakes in chocolate crispy cakes to boost fiber intake.

Make sure children take drinks with them when they exercise.

Ingredients for
Lemon barley water

- 3 ½ oz. pearl barley
- rind and juice of 2 lemons
- 4 cups cold water
- start with two teaspoons sugar or honey, and add to taste

For ideas on how to make fruit smoothies, see page 63.

Ingredients for
Ice-cream float

- scoop of vanilla ice cream
- 2 tablespoons pureed fruit
- a little sparkling mineral water (chilled)

Drinks and shakes

With so many child-tempting, sugar-laden drinks around, it's good to have a few alternatives on hand that will satisfy children's thirst for something more interesting than just water or milk. Some of these drinks get more fruit into children's diets, and the milk shakes and ice-cream float can double as desserts.

Lemon barley water

1. Rinse the barley in boiling water. (This will help to make the drink clearer.)
2. Pour into a saucepan, and add the lemon rind and cold water. Bring to a boil and simmer for 20 minutes.
3. Strain through a sieve into a large container.
4. Add the lemon juice and sugar, stirring until dissolved.
5. Chill in the refrigerator before serving and use within 24 hours.

Lemon barley water can be served with ice and lemon slices.

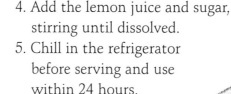

Ice-cream float

You can monitor the sugar content of this drink by making your own ice cream (see page 112).

1. Put the ice cream and pureed fruit in a tall glass.
2. Fill to the top with sparkling mineral water, pouring slowly, as it will fizz up. The ice cream should float to the top. Serve with straws.

Fruity milk shake

If bananas aren't popular in your house, just leave them out of this recipe. The banana helps to thicken and sweeten the drink, but the ice cream will do this too. Use homemade ice cream, if possible, to cut down on sugar.

Ingredients for Fruity milk shake

- 1 cup milk
- scoop of vanilla ice cream
- 1 banana (peeled)
- 5 strawberries (stalks removed)

1. Pour the milk into a blender and add the ice cream, banana and strawberries. Blend until frothy.
2. Serve in tall glasses with a straw.

Bananas are useful for thickening milk shakes and smoothies.

You could try replacing the strawberries with raspberries or blueberries.

Hand-held blenders are useful for mixing milk shakes.

Chocolate milk shake

Use cocoa powder rather than hot-chocolate mix for this recipe, as it doesn't contain any sugar. The sweetness will come from the ice cream. For an even healthier option, replace some of the ice cream with a banana.

Ingredients for Chocolate milk shake

- 1 cup milk
- 1 heaped teaspoon cocoa powder
- scoop of vanilla ice cream

1. Warm the milk in a saucepan.
2. Pour into a blender with the cocoa powder and ice cream and blend.
3. Serve in mugs.

Cocoa is high in antioxidants and the milk counts as one serving of dairy.

Fruit compotes and fools

A fool is made of cooked, pureed fruit that is strained, chilled and folded into whipped cream. A compote is a puree made from fruit.

Red berry compote

Strawberries, raspberries and blueberries work well here but you can use any berries, fresh or frozen.

1. Rinse the berries well and place them in a heavy-bottomed saucepan with the sugar and water.
2. Warm gradually over low heat.
3. Allow to reach simmering point and remove from the heat when the skins begin to burst.
4. Pass through a sieve to remove any seeds.

Ingredients for
Red berry compote

• 1 lb. berries
(stalks and leaves
removed)
• 2 tablespoons sugar
• 3 tablespoons water

Compotes are delicious served with the ice cream recipe on page 112. They can also be added to yogurt, smoothies, crumbles, cakes and fools.

Use the back of a wooden spoon to rub the compote through the sieve.

Summer fruit compote

Ingredients for
Summer fruit compote

• 4 nectarines (or peaches)
• 6 plums
• 6 apricots
• 1 tablespoon sugar

1. Preheat the oven to 350°F.
2. Remove the pits from the fruit.
3. Cut the nectarines into six slices, the plums into quarters and the apricots into halves.
4. Place the fruit on a baking tray, sprinkle with the sugar and cook, uncovered, in the oven for 25–30 minutes.
5. Pour into a blender, along with the juices, and blend until smooth. Chill in the refrigerator before serving.

Apricot fool

Ingredients for
Apricot fool (serves 4)

- 1 lb. 5 oz. ripe apricots
  (halved and pitted)
- juice of 1 large orange
- 1/3 cup sugar
- 2 cinnamon sticks (broken)
- 16 oz. low-fat plain yogurt
- zest of 1 lemon

A fool is a dessert made from pureed fruit and custard or cream.

Useful tip

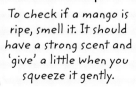

To check if a mango is ripe, smell it. It should have a strong scent and 'give' a little when you squeeze it gently.

1. Put the apricots, orange juice, sugar and cinnamon sticks in a saucepan.
2. Cover and cook gently for about 15 minutes, until the apricots are very soft.
2. Remove the cinnamon sticks and set the mixture aside to cool.
3. Spoon the yogurt into a bowl and stir in the lemon zest.
4. Gently fold most of the cooled apricot mixture into the yogurt.
5. Spoon into 4 serving glasses and top with the remaining apricot mixture.

Mango fool

The cream, coconut milk and yogurt make this recipe fairly high in fat, so serve this Caribbean dessert as an occasional treat when you can get really ripe mangoes.

Ingredients for
Mango fool (serves 4)

- flesh of 2 ripe mangoes
  (chopped)
- juice of 1 lemon (or lime)
- 5 oz. plain yogurt
- 4–5 teaspoons coconut milk
- 1/2 cup whipping cream

1. Put the mango flesh in a blender and blend until smooth. Pour into a bowl.
2. Pour in the lemon juice, yogurt and coconut milk.
3. In a separate bowl, whisk the cream until it thickens – but don't whisk it so much that it forms peaks.
4. Gently fold the cream into the mango mixture.
5. Pour into bowls or glasses and put them in the refrigerator to chill.

A crumble topping doesn't take long to make.

Crumbles

A fruit crumble can be made from various different fruits or a combination of them. You make the basic topping from flour, butter and sugar, but you can also add chopped nuts, seeds and oats. The sweetness of the crumble contrasts well with the slightly tart fruit.

Apple crumble

Apples, peaches and plums can all be prepared in the same way for this recipe, but if you use plums or peaches, remember to remove the pits before cooking.

Ingredients for
Apple crumble (serves 4)

- 2 lbs. cooking apples
  (peeled and cored)
- 4 tablespoons sugar
- 1 3/4 cup all-purpose flour
- 1/3 cup butter (cubed)

1. Preheat the oven to 375°F.
2. Roughly chop the apples, place in an oven-proof dish and cook in the oven for about 25 minutes.
3. Stir in 2 tablespoons of the sugar.
4. Put the flour and butter in a mixing bowl and use your fingertips to rub them together to make crumbs (or use a food processor for this).
5. Stir in the remainder of the sugar.
6. Scatter the topping over the cooked apples.
7. Return to the oven and cook for about 30 minutes, until the top is golden.

Using apple as a base, try adding strawberries, pears, blackberries or apricots.

Even young children can
help make a crumble.

- You could use half and half all-purpose flour and whole-wheat flour for the crumble topping.

- You could add 1/2 cup (2 oz.) of chopped walnuts, hazelnuts, sesame seeds, ground almonds or rolled oats at step 5.

Stewed fruit crumble

Ingredients for
Stewed fruit crumble
(serves 4)

- 10 oz. dried fruit
- 1 cup apple juice
- 1 lb. cooking apples
- 3 tablespoons sugar
- 1 ³/₄ cup all-purpose flour
- ¹/₃ cup butter (cubed)

In this variation on the apple crumble recipe, you replace half the apples with dried fruit.

1. Place the dried fruit in a saucepan, pour over the apple juice and bring to a boil.
2. Cover and simmer for about 30–45 minutes.
3. Cook the apples as outlined in the apple crumble recipe (steps 1–3), but only adding 1 tablespoon of sugar.
4. Stir the apples into the dried fruit. Check the sweetness and add a little sugar to taste, if necessary.
5. Follow steps 4–5 to make your crumble topping.
6. Arrange the fruit on the bottom of an oven-proof dish, sprinkle the topping over and bake it in the oven at 400°F for about 30 minutes, or until golden.

Any dried fruit can be used for this recipe, such as apricots, prunes, figs and berries.

You can also make a crumble with fresh, uncooked fruit. The crumbles in the photo were made with raspberries and peaches.

Useful tip

If you use a food processor to make the topping, don't mix for too long, or you'll end up with a solid lump of pastry.

Fruit salads and gelatin

Fruit salads and gelatin are another way to get more fruit into the diet and you can try out different combinations. You can also add canned or dried fruit soaked in fruit juice.

Tropical fruit salad

Ingredients for
Tropical fruit salad (serves 4)

- 1 small pineapple
- 2 mangoes
- 2 bananas
- 20 seedless grapes
- juice of 1 lemon
- juice of 1 orange

1. Chop the pineapple, mangoes and bananas into equal-sized pieces. Put them in a big bowl and add the grapes.
2. Squeeze over the lemon juice, which will help to prevent the fruit from turning brown.
3. Add the orange juice and stir well.
4. Serve by itself or with low-fat yogurt.

Show older children
how to prepare
fruit using a small,
sharp knife.

Summer fruit salad

Ingredients for
Summer fruit salad (serves 4)

- 2 eating apples
- juice of 1 lemon
- 3 1/2 oz. blueberries
- 3 1/2 oz. raspberries
- 3 1/2 oz. strawberries
- juice of 1 orange

1. Peel and chop the apples into thin slices, then chop these in half widthways. Put them in a dish and cover with lemon juice to prevent browning.
2. Add the blueberries, raspberries and strawberries.
3. Pour in the orange juice and mix carefully.
4. Refrigerate and serve by itself or with low-fat yogurt or whipped topping.

Homemade gelatin

Ingredients for
Homemade gelatin
(serves 4)

- 2 cups apple juice
- 1 package gelatin

Instant gelatin contains added sugar and coloring, so it's better to make your own.

Useful tip

Vegetarians don't eat gelatin. A good substitute is powdered agar-agar which is available at health-food stores.

You can use any fruit juice for this recipe – orange and raspberry both work well. You can also pour the liquid gelatin over fresh or canned fruit, but drain off any extra juice from the can first, as this will keep the gelatin from setting. Use unflavored gelatin.

1. Follow the package instructions for making gelatin, using the apple juice as your liquid.
2. Pour into bowls and allow to set in the refrigerator for a few hours before serving.

If you use a gelatin mold, lightly oil the inside before you pour in the gelatin to keep it from sticking.

Strawberry pudding

Ingredients for
Strawberry pudding
(serves 4)

- 8 oz. strawberries (stalks removed)
- 2/3 cup vanilla or strawberry yogurt
- 1/2 package plain gelatin

1. Blend the strawberries in a blender until smooth.
2. Pour into a bowl and stir in the yogurt.
3. Follow the package instructions for making gelatin, using the strawberry yogurt mixture as your liquid.
4. Pour into bowls and put into the refrigerator to set, but at the point when the gelatin begins to firm up, remove from the refrigerator and whisk vigorously.
5. Return to the refrigerator to set fully.
6. Turn out onto a plate and top with a few fresh strawberry halves.

Useful tip

Remove ice cream or frozen yogurt from the freezer 30 minutes before serving, to give it time to soften.

Ice cream and fruit pops

Commercial ice cream treats are often bulked up using vegetable oils and sugar, and even fruit pops made with fruit juice are usually high in sugar. Making your own allows you to cut out the oil and the sugar content. You don't need an ice cream maker for these recipes.

Try freezing fruit juice in ice-cube trays to make fruity ice cubes.

Homemade ice pops

To make ice pops you'll need some molds. Pour fresh fruit juice, fruit compote or diluted pureed fruit into them and put in the freezer for a few hours until the pops are solid. Hold the molds under warm water to help release the pops.

When strawberries are in season, you could freeze some to offer to children as healthy sweet treats.

You can buy plastic popsicle molds in the kitchen section of a grocery store.

Vanilla ice cream

Ingredients for Vanilla ice cream (serves 4)

- 1 cup heavy cream
- juice of 1 lemon
- 2 teaspoons vanilla
- 2 tablespoons honey

1. Mix all the ingredients together in a blender.
2. Pour into a plastic container and freeze.
3. After about 2 hours, before it is fully frozen, remove from the freezer and mash with a fork. (This will help to prevent any ice crystals from forming.)
4. Return to the freezer for 4 hours, or until firm.

Frozen yogurt

You can make this in exactly the same way as ice cream, but replace the cream with yogurt, which makes it lower in fat.

Experiment with adding fruit to ice cream or frozen yogurt.

Brown bread ice cream

Blend two slices of whole-wheat bread in a food processor to make crumbs, and toast in the oven until crisp. Follow the vanilla ice-cream recipe, but stir the toasted crumbs into the cream mixture after step 1 and leave it in the refrigerator for about an hour, to give the toasted crumbs time to soften, before continuing with the recipe.

It sounds improbable, but brown bread really does make delicious ice cream.

Raspberry ice cream

Ingredients for
Raspberry ice cream (serves 4)
• 8oz. fresh raspberries
• ½ cup powdered sugar (sifted)
• 4 tablespoons vanilla yogurt
• ½ cup heavy whipping cream

1. Mash the raspberries with a fork and stir in the powdered sugar, then the yogurt.
2. In a separate bowl, whip the cream until it thickens, then fold it into the raspberry mixture.
3. Pour into a plastic container and freeze for 2 hours.
4. Remove from the freezer and mash with a fork.
5. Return to the freezer for 4 hours, or until firm.

You could decorate raspberry ice cream with a sprig of mint and some raspberries.

Sponge cakes

There's not much you can do about the fat content of cakes. You can substitute low-fat margarine for butter, but the taste will be impaired. While cakes do contain a lot of fat, there is also nutritional value from the eggs (protein), and any fruits included.

Don't forget that icing a cake adds greatly to its sugar content.

If a cake sinks, serve it with some ice cream as a special dessert.

Try to make sure no eggshell drops into the cake mixture, if you crack eggs straight into the bowl.

Fruit sponge cake

This recipe needs to be made in a pan with a fixed bottom or in an oven-proof dish, so the fruit can't leak out while it is cooking.

Ingredients for Fruit sponge cake (serves 4)
- 1 lb. (about 3 medium) plums
- 2 tablespoons water
- 3/4 cup butter
- 3/4 cup sugar
- 3 eggs (beaten)
- 1 1/2 cups self-rising flour (sifted)

You could replace the plums with pieces of pear or apple.

1. Preheat the oven to 350°F.
2. Cut the plums in half and remove the pits. Put them in a saucepan and add the water.
3. Heat gently until the plums are soft-cooked. Spoon with the juices into an oven-proof dish.
4. Cream the butter and sugar in a bowl. Beat in the eggs, then gently fold in the sifted flour.
5. Spoon the mixture over the plums. Don't worry if it doesn't cover them evenly; it will spread out in the oven.
6. Bake for 25–30 minutes, or until golden brown. Serve with frozen yogurt, whipped cream, pudding or yogurt.

Carrot cupcakes

Ingredients for
Carrot cupcakes (makes 12)

- 1 large carrot (peeled and
  finely grated)
- 2 eggs (beaten)
- 6 tablespoons canola oil
- 1 cup brown sugar
- ¹/₂ cup self-rising flour
- ¹/₃ cup whole-wheat flour
- ¹/₂ teaspoon baking
  powder
- 1 teaspoon ground
  cinnamon
- 1 teaspoon ground ginger

1. Preheat the oven to 375°F.
2. Put twelve paper baking cups into a cupcake tray.
3. In a bowl beat together the sugar and oil for 1 minute. Add the eggs, a little at a time. Then add the grated carrot and stir well.
4. Sift both flours, the baking powder, and the cinnamon and ginger into the mixture. (Pour any bran left in the sieve into the bowl.)
5. Use a wooden spoon to fold together very gently, until well mixed.
6. Spoon into the baking cups and bake for 15 minutes.
7. Remove from the oven and lift onto a wire rack to cool, before icing with cream-cheese icing:

Cream-cheese icing

Ingredients for
Cream-cheese icing

- 3 oz. low-fat cream cheese
- 1 cup powdered sugar
- 1 teaspoon vanilla
- 2 oz. dried tropical fruit

1. Mix together the cream cheese and vanilla.
2. Beat in the powdered sugar until smooth.
3. Use a knife to spread the frosting over the top of each cupcake and decorate with the chopped fruit.

Top the cupcakes with
whole pecans if you prefer.

Other sweet treats

There's nothing wrong with a sweet treat once in a while, but, as always, it's healthier to make your own.

Fruit scones

Ingredients for
Fruit scones
(makes about 12)

- 4 tablespoons butter
- 1 cup, minus 2 tablespoons self-rising flour (sifted)
- ³/₄ cup whole-wheat flour (sifted)
- 2 tablespoons raisins
- ¹/₂ cup milk
- ¹/₄ cup sugar

1. Preheat the oven to 425°F.
2. Rub the butter into the flour and add the sugar.
3. Mix in the raisins, then add the milk, a little at a time, stirring with a knife.
4. Flour your hands and gently knead the mixture into a ball. (Add a little more milk if it is too dry and crumbly.)
5. Sprinkle flour onto the work surface and roll out the dough until it is about 1 inch thick.
6. Cut out the scones with a small round cookie cutter and place on a greased baking tray. Bake near the top of the oven for 12–15 minutes.

Fruit scones go well with strawberry jam.

Children often like making scones.

Chocolate bran-flake cakes

Ingredients for
Chocolate bran-flake cakes
(makes about 12)

- 8 oz. milk chocolate
- 6 oz. bran flakes

1. Break the chocolate into pieces and place into a heat-proof bowl over a pan of simmering water.
2. Wait until the chocolate has melted fully before stirring.
3. Remove from the heat and add the bran flakes, stirring gently until completely covered in chocolate.
4. Spoon the mixture into paper baking cups and allow to stand for about 1 hour, while the chocolate sets.

Macaroons

Ingredients for
Macaroons (makes 20)

• baking parchment
• 2 egg whites
• 6 oz. ground almonds
• 1/2 cup sugar

This recipe uses ground almonds. If you can't find ground, get slivered and use a mortar and pestle or food processor to grind them into a fine powder.

1. Grease and line a medium sized baking tray with baking parchment.
2. Separate the eggs by cracking them over a bowl and pouring the yolk from one half of the shell to the other, allowing the egg white to fall away into the bowl.
3. Put the yolks in a cup, cover with clingfilm and store in the refrigerator, as they are not used in this recipe.
4. Whisk the whites in the bowl until they form stiff peaks. (Make sure there is no fat present in the bowl – such as yolk drips – or it won't work.)
5. Fold in the almonds and sugar and roll into 20 little balls. Place each one on the baking parchment and flatten.
6. Bake in the oven at 350°F for 15 minutes, or until the macaroons are golden.

You could use the leftover egg yolks to make homemade custard, or add them to an omelet (see page 60).

Fruity oatmeal squares

Ingredients for
Fruity oatmeal squares
(makes 20)

• 2 eating apples (cut into small chunks)
• 1 1/2 sticks butter
• 2/3 cup brown sugar
• 2 tablespoons honey
• 1 cup (8 oz.) quick-cook oats
• 1/3 cup raisins
• 2 oz. hazelnuts (chopped)

1. Grease a 7 x 11 inch baking tray.
2. Put the apple chunks in a saucepan with 1 tablespoon of butter. Cook over low heat for 10 minutes, until soft.
3. Add the rest of the butter, sugar and honey and heat gently until melted.
4. Take off the heat and stir in the oats, raisins and hazelnuts. Pour the mixture into the baking tray and smooth to the edges.
5. Bake in the oven at 350°F for 20–30 minutes, until golden brown. Leave to cool and cut into small squares.

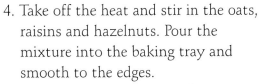

Fruity oatmeal squares are easy for children to make.

Jammy cookies

For these sweet treats you'll need some small shaped cutters as well as a 2 inch round cutter.

1. Preheat the oven to 350°F.
2. Beat the butter and sugar in a bowl until smooth.
3. Stir in the orange rind, then the egg, a little at a time.
4. Add the ground almonds and then the flour.
   Mix together with your hands to form a dough.
5. Wrap the dough in clingfilm and put in the refrigerator for 30 minutes to chill.
6. Sprinkle some flour on a clean worktop. Using a rolling pin, roll out the dough so it is about 1/8 inch thick.
7. Use a 2 inch round cutter to cut out lots of circles.
8. Use small shaped cutters to cut holes in the middle of half of the circles.
9. Place all of the circles on a greased baking tray and bake for 15 minutes.
10. When cool, spread jam on top of the whole cookies.
    Place a cut-out cookie on top and press gently together.

Ingredients for
Jammy cookies
(makes about 10)

- ½ cup butter (softened)
- ⅓ cup sugar
- rind of 1 orange
- 1 egg (beaten)
- 2 tablespoons ground almonds
- 1 ¾ cups all-purpose flour (sifted)
- 1 tablespoon corn flour
- 8 tablespoons jam

You could use a large shaped cutter to make star shaped cookies, if you prefer.

You could use some different kinds of jam in these cookies.

118

Useful information

In this final section of the book, you'll find more detailed information about specific food allergies, as well as some general cooking tips and a useful guide to measurement conversions. There is also some information about websites to visit where you can find out more about healthy eating for young children.

At a glance

The major allergy-causing foods
and symptoms to look out for

Conversion tables for quantities in recipes

Quick tips for healthy eating

Useful websites to visit

Specific food allergies

These pages contain information about specific food allergies. For more
general information about food allergies and intolerance, see pages 38–39.

Allergy or intolerance	Possible symptoms	Caused by	Will my child grow out of it?	Related foods to avoid	Additional notes
Milk allergy	Often mild and can affect any part of the body: rashes, diarrhea, vomiting, stomach cramps, difficulty breathing, in severe cases anaphylactic reactions*.	Hypersensitivity to a number of the proteins found in cow's milk.	Children usually grow out of it by the age of 3, but about a fifth of children who have it will still be allergic as adults.	All types of milk and milk-based products, including powdered milk, buttermilk and butter.	Talk to your doctor or dietician before eliminating milk from a child's diet, as milk is an important source of protein and calcium.
Milk intolerance (also called milk protein intolerance)	Eczema, vomiting, diarrhea, stomach cramps, but NOT hives or breathing problems.	Hypersensitivity to a number of the proteins found in cow's milk.	Children often grow out of it by the time they start school.	All types of milk and milk-based products, including powdered milk, buttermilk and butter.	See above.
Lactose intolerance	Stomach cramps, bloating and diarrhea.	A lack of the enzyme lactase in the body, which is needed to break down lactose, the sugars found in cow's milk.	Can affect children (especially babies that are born prematurely), but generally affects adults, as lactose production falls as you get older.	All types of milk and some milk-based products.	See above. Sufferers may be able to eat cheese and yogurt, as cheese contains much less lactose than milk.
Egg allergy	Rashes, diarrhea, vomiting, stomach cramps, difficulty breathing, in severe cases anaphylactic reactions*.	Hypersensitivity to three proteins in egg white: ovomucoid, ovalbumin and conalbumin.	About half of children with this allergy grow out of it by the age of 3–5.	Egg-based pasta, mayonnaise, custard, pancakes, meringue, most cakes and cookies, many ice creams (recipes on pages 112–113 are fine).	Cooking can destroy some of the allergens, but not all, so some children may be able to eat cooked eggs, but not raw ones (ex. in mayonnaise).
Nut allergy	Tingling or swelling in the mouth or throat, itching, asthma, vomiting, diarrhea. Can cause anaphylactic reactions*.	Hypersensitivity to a number of proteins in nuts.	Usually lasts a lifetime.	Walnuts, almonds, pecans, hazelnuts, macadamia nuts, cashews, Brazil nuts, nut oil, anything made in a factory where nuts are used.	Always check food labels carefully, as nuts can appear in trace amounts, which is often enough to cause a reaction.

*See page 39.

Allergy or intolerance	Possible symptoms	Caused by	Will my child grow out of it?	Related foods to avoid	Additional notes
Peanut (also called monkey nut or groundnut) allergy	Hives, swelling of the tongue or throat, vomiting, breathing problems. Can cause very severe anaphylactic reactions*. Symptoms appear almost immediately.	Hypersensitivity to a number of proteins in peanuts.	Appears most commonly in the first 3 years of life and usually lasts a lifetime, although some children may grow out of it.	Peanut oil (also called groundnut oil), anything made in a factory where peanuts are used.	Using a knife that has already been used to chop peanuts can be enough to cause a reaction, or even just being near someone eating them. The allergens are not destroyed by cooking.
Soy allergy	Rashes, diarrhea, vomiting, stomach cramps and breathing difficulties, in very rare cases can cause anaphylactic reactions*.	Hypersensitivity to the proteins in soy beans.	Most children grow out of it by the age of 2, but occasionally continues into adulthood.	Tofu, TVP (textured vegetable protein), soy sauce, soy milk. Soy is also often used in processed foods, such as margarine, bakery goods, pasta and drinks.	Some people with soy allergies also react to milk, peanuts, peas, lentils and chickpeas.
Wheat allergy	Rashes, asthma, diarrhea, vomiting, stomach cramps and breathing difficulties, in very rare cases can cause anaphylactic reactions*. Symptoms occur in minutes.	Hypersensitivity to gliadin, albumin, globulin or glutenin, the proteins found in wheat.	A fairly rare condition. Usually develops in childhood.	Bread, pasta, pizza, pastry, cakes (unless specifically wheat-free varieties). Wheat is often added to sausages, burgers, sauces and batters.	Wheat allergy is different to coeliac disease (see below). Look for products labeled 'wheat-free', which is different than 'gluten-free'.
Gluten intolerance (also called coeliac or celiac disease)	Bloating, diarrhea, weight loss, fatigue and, in severe cases, eventually malnutrition. If left uncontrolled, can lead to anemia and growth problems in children. Symptoms take hours or even days to emerge.	Hypersensitivity of the gut lining to gluten, a protein found in cereal grains, such as wheat, rye, and barley.	Can develop at any age and usually lasts a lifetime.	Anything containing wheat, rye, barley, etc; pasta, pizza, pastry, cakes – unless gluten-free varieties. Gluten is also often added to sausages, burgers, sauces and batters.	This condition often runs in families and many people don't realize they have it. Look for products labeled 'gluten-free', which is different than 'wheat-free'.

Read food labels carefully. For more information, see page 34.

Measurements and conversions

Here are some useful cooking conversions:

3 teaspoons = 1 tablespoon
4 tablespoons = ¼ cup
5 ⅓ tablespoons = ⅓ cup
8 tablespoons = ½ cup
10 ⅔ tablespoons = ⅔ cup
12 tablespoons = ¾ cup
16 tablespoons = 1 cup

1 tablespoon = ½ fluid ounce
1 cup = 8 fluid ounces
1 cup = ½ pint
2 cups = 1 pint
4 cups = 1 quart
2 pints = 1 quart
4 quarts = 1 gallon

1 quart = 1 liter

Cooking tips

There are many tips, tricks and simple techniques that can make kitchen tasks easier or help to improve results. Some are included in the recipes in this book, but below are a few more which you may find useful:

• To stop dough from sticking to your hands, the worktop, or a rolling pin, dust them with a little flour.

• When whisking egg whites, use an electric mixer or egg beater. (If you don't, the whites won't go light and fluffy.)

• Cut vegetables into equal-sized pieces, so they cook evenly.

• If you don't have a blender or food processor for making breadcrumbs, use a grater instead. Slightly stale bread works best — or lightly toast a fresh slice.

• If a recipe lists softened butter, take it out of the refrigerator 30 minutes before using it.

• Fillets of fish shouldn't have any bones in them, but it's a good idea to check anyway, in case any have been missed.

• When you're cooking something in an oven, put it on the middle shelf, unless the recipe says otherwise.

• When using a broiler, position food about 3 inches below the heat source. Any closer risks burning, and any lower means the food takes longer to cook.

• If you're having trouble serving ice cream, dip the scoop or spoon in some hot water and try again.

Oven temperatures

Oven temperatures can vary considerably from oven to oven, and sometimes the temperature on the dial doesn't precisely match the actual temperature inside the oven, so the times and temperatures listed for the recipes in this book may need adjusting slightly to suit your own oven. Below is a conversion table of oven temperatures which you may also find useful:

160°C	325°F	gas mark 3	Moderate
180°C	350°F	gas mark 4	Moderate
190°C	375°F	gas mark 5	Moderately hot
200°C	400°F	gas mark 6	Moderately hot
220°C	425°F	gas mark 7	Hot
230°C	450°F	gas mark 8	Hot

Convection ovens are usually hotter than other ovens, so check the instruction book to see if you need to lower a temperature. As a rough guide, it's usual to reduce the temperature listed by 50°F and the cooking times roughly by 10 minutes for every hour of cooking when using a convection oven.

Storing food

Store breads, cakes and pastries in an airtight container and keep food well covered to keep flies away and prevent it from drying out. Anything containing fresh cream should be served immediately or kept in the refrigerator.

For more information about storing food safely, see page 47.

Internet links

The internet is a good source of information on healthy eating. At the Usborne Quicklinks Website there are links to lots of websites you may find useful and other things you can download. To visit the sites, go to **www.usborne-quicklinks.com** and type the keywords 'children and food'.

Here are some of the things you can do via Usborne Quicklinks:

- *Watch video clips of chefs showing how to prepare delicious recipes.*

- *Use an online weights and measures calculator to convert the measures in recipes.*

- *Find more information and advice for children with food allergies.*

- *Discover which foods are in season at which times of year in your area.*

Internet safety

The websites recommended in Usborne Quicklinks are regularly reviewed. However, the content of a website may change at any time and Usborne Publishing is not responsible for the content or availability of websites other than its own.

General index

Recipe index

With thanks to...

Staff and pupils at Long Ditton Infant and Nursery School;
Staff and pupils at Long Ditton St Mary's School;
Lower Roundhurst Farm, West Sussex;
Fiona Patchett, Abigail Wheatley, Emily Bone, Kate Davies,
Lucy Beckett-Bowman and Hazel Maskell for recipe testing;
Sam Taplin for proofreading and indexing;
Claire Masset for picture and website research

Photo credits:

The publishers are grateful to the following for permission to reproduce material:
p20 © JUPITERIMAGES/Brand X/Alamy; p43 © Bloomimage/Corbis; p53
© Photolibrary Group/Digital Vision; p60 © David Loftus Limited/Stockfood

Additional illustrations: Dubravka Kolanovic

Digital imaging: Keith Furnival

Americanization: Carrie Armstrong and Jessica Greenwell